CITIES IN CRISIS

INQUIRY INTO CRUCIAL AMERICAN PROBLEMS
Series Editor JACK R. FRAENKEL

CITIES IN CRISIS:

Decay or Renewal?
Second Edition

Rudie W. Tretten

Vice Principal for Guidance
Jefferson High School
Daly City, California

PRENTICE-HALL, INC., ENGLEWOOD CLIFFS, N.J.

Photo Credits

Wide World Photos, viii, 34, 43 (top, middle), 60, 93, 115; Culver Pictures, Inc., 4; The Bettmann Archive, Inc., 13; Fujihira from Monkmeyer Press Photo Service, 24; Joel Gordon, 28; Rogers from Monkmeyer Press Photo Service, 42; © Leo Stashin from Rapho/Photo Researchers, Inc., 43 (bottom); Hays from Monkmeyer Press Photo Service, 47; Robert Crawford from dpi, 66; © Alon Reininger from dpi, 78; Secolow & Harte from dpi, 88; Ema from dpi, 89; Otis Elevator Co., 109.

Cover designed by Diane Kachalsky.

Library of Congress Cataloging in Publication Data
TRETTEN RUDIE W   comp.
   Cities in crisis.
   (Inquiry into crucial American problems)
   Bibliography: p.
   1. Cities and towns—United States. I. Title.
HT123.T68 1977   301.36'3'0973   76-20619
ISBN 0-13-134577-X
ISBN 0-13-134569-9 pbk.

Prentice-Hall International, Inc.,
London
Prentice-Hall of Australia, Pty. Ltd.,
Sydney
Prentice-Hall of Canada, Ltd.,
Toronto
Prentice-Hall of India Private Ltd.,
New Delhi
Prentice-Hall of Japan, Inc.,
Tokyo

PREFACE

The series INQUIRY INTO CRUCIAL AMERICAN PROBLEMS focuses upon a number of important contemporary social and political issues. Each book presents an in-depth study of a particular problem, selected because of its pressing intrusion into the minds and consciences of most Americans today.

A number of divergent viewpoints, from a wide variety of different *kinds* of sources, encourage discussion and reflection, and help students to realize that the same problem may be viewed from a number of different vantage points. Of major concern throughout is a desire to help students realize that honest individuals may differ in their views.

After a short introductory chapter, Chapter Two presents a brief historical and contemporary background on the central issue. The chapters that follow explore the issue in detail. A conscientious effort has been made to avoid endorsing any one viewpoint as the "right" viewpoint, or to judge the arguments of particular individuals or organizations. Conclusions are not drawn for students. Instead, a variety of positions are presented, along with open-ended questions and involving activities, so that students can arrive at and evaluate their own conclusions.

Great care has been taken to make these books substantive, highly interesting to students, and readable. Whenever possible, dialogues involving or descriptions showing actual people responding and reacting to problematic situations are presented. Briefly, each book

- presents divergent, conflicting views on the issue under consideration;

- gives as many perspectives and dimensions on the issue as space permits;

- presents articles on a variety of reading levels;

- deals with real people involved in situations of concern to them;

- includes questions which encourage thought about and discussion of the various viewpoints expressed;

- includes activities that involve students and lead to further consideration of the problems presented;

- provides cartoons, photographs, and other illustrations to help students arrive at a more complete understanding of the issue under study.

JACK R. FRAENKEL
Series Editor

v

CONTENTS

1
INTRODUCTION

Imagine yourself in a spaceship hovering above any one of the large American cities. You and the crew and the group of tourists with you are staring toward the earth attempting to make sense of what you see. Imagine, too, the following conversation with the guide:

> *Guide:* Below us now is a characteristic settlement of earthlings. It is called a city.
>
> *Tourist 1:* But it is so crowded. Look at all of those people living piled up together. Doesn't that cause problems?
>
> *Guide:* Oh, yes. Crowding causes all sorts of problems—crime, disease, psychological difficulties—but all over the earth cities are growing rapidly.
>
> *Tourist 2:* But in this city it seems that there are some divisions among the people. See, look at the center of the city—all of the people seem to have dark skins while away from the center the skins of the people are lighter.
>
> *Guide:* Yes, that is a peculiarity of the cities of this country, the United States. Skin color seems to mean a lot to these people.
>
> *Tourist 3:* Something funny down there. Look how our view is being obscured by smoke and dust. Don't they have to breathe the air?
>
> *Guide:* Oh, yes, and drink the water too. Notice how dirty the water seems to be. And how they seem to be putting various waste matter into the water. They have to drink that.
>
> *Tourist 1:* They all seem to get into small vehicles, move for a while and stop. They don't go anywhere.
>
> *Guide:* Transportation for so many people is a real problem.
>
> *Tourist 2:* Look at the center of the city. The buildings seem to be either very high and new or low and old and dilapidated. And look at those large areas in the middle of the city where everything has been torn down. What is all that about?
>
> *Guide:* The high buildings in the center of the city are homes for the wealthy and offices for the powerful decision makers. The old and decrepit buildings are the homes of the poor. The open spaces are areas where the houses of the poor have been torn down. Sometime in the future new housing and offices will be built there.

Tourist 3: It certainly doesn't look like a pleasant place. Why do people live in cities if they are like what we see?

Guide: People come together in cities to live the good life.

"To live the good life." Do our cities allow their citizens to enjoy the "good life" that so many advertisements seem to promise? Cities are centers of humanity's great cultural achievements; cities mean job opportunities; cities have great universities; cities offer excitement and action; but do cities provide "the good life"?

There is little doubt that America's cities, and those of many other nations, are in deep trouble. Crime, overcrowding, pollution, racial polarization, personal anxiety, and fiscal problems have become hallmarks of American urban life. Yet cities and the suburban areas that surround them continue to attract more residents. By the year 2000 it is estimated that over 230 million Americans will be living in urban areas in the United States.

Some of the most pressing problems which confront city dwellers—as well as the rest of us—are these:

1. *Housing.* The central sections of many cities are old and dilapidated. Into these areas have flooded millions of recent migrants from the South, from rural areas, from Latin America and Asia. City officials are faced with the problem of finding adequate housing for these new residents. Many of the newcomers to the city have language and other educational difficulties which limit the types of jobs they can obtain. This, in turn, limits their ability to earn enough to afford adequate housing.

2. *Transportation.* While the recent energy crisis has focused attention on gasoline supplies and the need to develop rapid transit systems to conserve fuels, the automobile has been a problem in the city for a long time. More and more autos crowd streets and highways. Buildings are torn down to make room for parking lots. Short journeys to an airport often take longer than a 500-mile flight. The automobile may be outdated as a useful mover of people in and around cities.

3. *Pollution.* The air breathed by Americans has become increasingly contaminated with the waste matter from industry and motor vehicles. Increased demands for energy have led to relaxation of the regulations dealing with air pollution. Many major streams and lakes have been polluted and become dangerous to man and animals. While there has been evidence of improvement in recent years, the energy crisis is forcing the nation to a continuing series of choices and trade-offs between dirty energy sources and clean air and water.

4. *Planning.* Most cities have hired staffs of planners whose task is to create an orderly plan for development of the city. Difficulties arise over the enforcement of such plans. Cities are surrounded by suburbs which often have become small cities in themselves. The difficulties of the city spill over into the surrounding area, and the problems of the suburbs have become problems for the city. Only rarely do we find official governmental agencies charged with developing a master plan for an entire area. Increasingly citizens are demand-

ing the right to participate in the planning process, but our institutions have not provided methods for such participation.

The problems listed above do not exhaust the catalogue of dilemmas which cities face. In a book of this size, it is impossible to cover adequately all of the dilemmas created by increasing urbanization. The treatment here will deal primarily with the quality of city life—with what makes life in cities worth living. We shall consider the following questions in particular:

1. How can we create cities in which people can live together without fear?
2. How can adequate shelter be assured for all segments of American society?
3. How can a series of transportation systems be created to allow maximum convenience and safety?
4. How much are people willing to pay for the city's services and for clean air and water? Can the city support itself?
5. What should be the role of planning in urban areas?
6. What will life in America's cities be like in the year 2000?

2
THE CITY: PAST AND PRESENT

No one knows for certain when or how the first city developed. In all likelihood, it evolved from an earlier, smaller settlement. But, as they grew, the first cities added a new dimension and scale to human life. Bringing many people together in one place made it possible for some to specialize in the various arts and crafts necessary for survival. People began to develop administrative and organizational skills in order to govern the city's inhabitants.

It is probable that cities arose when it became possible to produce sufficient food so that some people could specialize in non-food-gathering pursuits. These nonagricultural experts came together to form cities and to provide a marketplace for a developing agricultural economy. Writing became a necessary aid to the growth of cities because records of ownership, taxes, and business transactions had to be kept. With the growth of writing systems there developed a new "educated" class capable of taking care of governmental and business affairs.

The first cities probably came into being about 5,500 years ago in the Fertile Crescent, that area of present-day Iraq which includes the valleys of the Tigris and Euphrates. There was a great deal of fertile land in the Tigris-Euphrates valley which could produce more food than the farmers and their families could consume, so they could trade food for other kinds of goods. The rivers formed a natural transportation system, which meant that trade could take place and that people could get to the city. The coming together of people from many places provided an adequate store of ideas and skills to create a city.

The first cities, with names like Eridu, Erech, and Ur, were very much alike. Each of the cities was headed by a king, who was also the high priest. These high priest-kings had absolute power of life and death over their subjects.

Between 3500 and 3000 B.C. technology underwent great changes, which led to the growth of more and greater cities. The potter's wheel, the draw loom, the sailing vessel, copper metalurgy, systems of writing, and the calendar all came into existence about this time. The resulting increased production and specialization induced more people to come to the city which, in turn, led to more technological change and greater division of labor among the residents. Cities began to expand and in time became empires.

The Greek city-states are possibly the most famous of the old cities. The struggles between Athens and Sparta for supremacy are a part of history texts throughout the Western world. Another famous city, Rome, at the height of its power and glory was so crowded that at one point the officials had to issue special regulations concerning chariot traffic. Yet Rome never exceeded between 300,000 and 1 million population. Today the sixth largest city in California has more than 300,000 residents.

The great explosion in the size of cities came with the industrial revolution. More specifically, it occurred during the last 100 years of that revolution. All the older industrialized nations and many emerging industrial societies are experiencing or have experienced a tremendous growth in their cities. In part this can be accounted for by the general increase in world population, and in part it represents a migration from rural areas to urban areas as people seek work and a better life.

In the United States, the growth of cities was slow until the last half of the nineteenth century. Then, fed by the increase of immigration from Europe, cities began to grow rapidly.

Between 1840 and 1900, the population of New York City increased from 312,000 to 3,437,000. In the same time period, Chicago went from 4,000 people to 1,700,000. Boston, Philadelphia, and Pittsburgh had similar growth patterns. In the 90 years from 1880 to 1970 the population of Los Angeles soared from 10,000 to 2,800,000.

At the same time that immigrants were filling the cities, there was a movement of people from the countryside to the urban areas of the nation. By 1920 over half of the American people lived in urban areas. Now over 70 percent of America lives in and around cities. By 1980, it is predicted that this will rise to 80 percent.

It is not only cities which have increased in size. Suburbs, particularly since World War II, have grown enormously. Two examples will illustrate this trend:

1. In 1947, the area which now houses Levittown, New York, had a single three-room schoolhouse with 37 pupils. By 1954, this six-square-mile area housed 70,000 people. The 37 pupils had increased by over 300 times, to 12,500.

2. In 1940, Daly City, California, which borders San Francisco on the south, had a population of about 10,000. By 1974, this had grown to over 70,000. San Mateo County, of which Daly City is a part, grew from 235,000 in 1950 to almost 600,000 by 1974.

Suburbs have continued to grow rapidly, but the growth of central cities has slowed. In some places cities are losing citizens. The chart below shows how cities have grown, and in some cases declined, over the years.

One explanation for the loss of population by some cities is that middle-class white families have left as more and more nonwhites have moved in. Increasingly the city has become the home of individuals who are very poor, often uneducated, often on welfare, and often discriminated against. The mid-

Rank	Cities	1970	1960	1950	1900	1850	1790
1	New York, N.Y.	7,894,862	7,781,984	7,891,957	3,437,202	696,115	49,401
	Bronx boro	1,471,701	1,424,815	1,451,277	200,507	8,032	1,781
	Brooklyn boro	2,602,012	2,627,319	2,738,175	1,166,582	138,882	4,495
	Manhattan boro	1,539,233	1,698,281	1,960,101	1,850,093	515,547	33,131
	Queens boro	1,987,174	1,809,578	1,550,849	152,999	18,593	6,159
	Richmond boro	295,443	221,991	191,555	67,021	15,061	3,835
2	Chicago, Ill.	3,369,359	3,550,404	3,620,962	1,698,575	29,963	—
3	Los Angeles, Calif.	2,809,596	2,479,015	1,970,358	102,479	1,610	—
4	Phila., Pa.	1,950,098	2,002,512	2,071,605	1,293,697	121,376	28,522
5	Detroit, Mich.	1,513,601	1,670,144	1,849,568	285,704	21,019	—
6	Houston, Tex.	1,232,802	938,219	596,163	44,633	2,396	—
7	Baltimore, Md.	905,759	939,024	949,708	508,957	169,054	13,503
8	Dallas, Tex.	844,401	679,684	434,462	42,638	—	—
9	Washington, D.C.	756,510	763,956	802,178	278,718	40,001	—
10	Cleveland, Ohio	750,879	876,050	914,808	381,768	17,034	—
11	Indianapolis, Ind.	744,743	476,258	427,173	169,164	8,091	—
12	Milwaukee, Wis.	717,372	741,324	637,392	285,315	20,061	—
13	San Francisco, Calif.	715,674	740,316	775,357	342,782	234,776	—
14	San Diego, Calif.	697,027	573,224	334,387	17,700	—	—
15	San Antonio, Tex.	654,153	587,718	408,442	53,321	3,488	—
16	Boston, Mass.	641,071	697,197	801,444	560,892	136,881	18,320
17	Memphis, Tenn.	623,530	497,524	396,000	102,320	8,841	—
18	St. Louis, Mo.	622,236	750,026	856,796	575,238	77,860	—
19	New Orleans, La.	593,471	627,525	570,445	287,104	116,375	—
20	Phoenix, Ariz.	581,562	439,170	106,818	5,544	—	—
21	Columbus, Ohio	540,025	471,316	375,901	125,560	17,882	—
22	Seattle, Wash.	530,831	557,087	467,591	80,671	—	—
23	Jacksonville, Fla.	528,865	201,030	204,517	28,429	1,045	—
24	Pittsburgh, Pa.	520,117	604,332	676,806	321,616	46,601	—
25	Denver, Colo.	514,678	493,887	415,786	133,859	—	—

Source: U.S. Bureau of the Census, *United States Statistical Abstract 1972*, p. 136.

dle-class flight from the city now includes middle-class minority-group citizens anxious to avoid the crowding, crime, and dirt of city life.

It must be emphasized that urban growth is occurring around the world. Latin America and Africa, two continents which Americans usually think of as rural in their life style, are experiencing tremendous urban growth. This naturally causes great problems for the nations of these continents since many of them do not have the industrial capacity to supply jobs for all those who come to the city looking for work. On the outskirts of many Latin American cities there are huge shantytowns, where the newcomers try to survive.

The United States has always had mixed feelings about cities. On the one hand, some writers (such as Walt Whitman) have written of the virtues of the city; on the other, the vast majority of American writers and intellectuals have expressed a deep mistrust of the city. In general, this mistrust forms a theme in American life. The poor girl goes to the city and is forced into a life of shame;

the country hick goes to the city and is sold a bridge; or the honest young man from the country becomes an unhappy and destroyed city dweller.

These myths from the past are still important today. It is difficult for cities to get adequate legislation passed in state legislatures. The national Congress still overrepresents rural areas, so that city problems often go begging for solution. Recent events have brought some changes, but cities still find themselves at a disadvantage.

The following selections give some indication of the mixed feelings of Americans about the city.

1. The Views of Thomas Jefferson*

Jefferson saw the farmer—not the city worker—as the salvation of the nation. Would you agree with him?

Those who labor in the earth are the chosen people of God . . . Corruption of morals in the mass of cultivators is a phenomenon of which no age or nation has furnished an example . . . but, generally speaking, the proportion which the aggregate of the other classes of citizens bears in any state to that of its husbandmen, is the proportion of its unsound to its healthy parts, and is a good enough barometer whereby to measure its degree of corruption. . . . The mobs of great cities add just so much to the support of pure government, as sores do to the strength of the human body.

What Do You Think? _____

Fewer and fewer Americans live on farms (approximately 8 percent and declining). Does this mean that the nation's morality is being corrupted? Explain your answer.

2. The Romance of City Life**

The poet Walt Whitman looked at a city and saw something more than the mobs. His poem "Mannahatta" expresses this view.

*I was asking for something specific and perfect for my city,
Whereupon lo! up sprang the aboriginal name.*

*Excerpted from Dumas Malone, *Jefferson, the Virginian* (Boston: Little, Brown & Co., 1948).
**From Walt Whitman, "Mannahatta," in *Leaves of Green* (1855). New York: New American Library, Mentor Edition.

Now I saw what there is in a name, a word, liquid, sane, unruly, musical, self-sufficient,
I see that the word of my city is that word from of old,
Because I see that word nested in nests of water-bays superb,
Rich, hemm'd thick all around with sailships and steamships, an island sixteen miles long, solid-founded,
Numberless crowded streets, high growths of iron, slender, strong, light, splendidly uprising toward clear skies,
Tides swift and ample, well loved by me, toward sundown,
The flowing sea-currents, the little islands, larger adjoining islands, the heights, the villas,
The countless masts, the white shore-streamers, the lighters, the ferryboats, the black sea-streamers well model'd,
The down-town streets, the jobbers' houses of business, the houses of business of the ship-merchants, and money-brokers, the river-streets,
Immigrants arriving, fifteen thousand in a week,
The carts hauling goods, the manly race of drivers of horses, the brown-faced sailors,
The summer air, the bright sun shining, and the sailing clouds aloft,
The winter snows, the sleigh-bells, the broken ice in the river, passing along up or down with the flood-tide or ebb-tide,
The mechanics of the city, the masters, well-form'd, beautiful-faced, looking you straight in the eyes,
Trottoirs throng'd, vehicles, Broadway, the women, the shops and shows,
A million people—manners free and superb—open voices—hospitality— the most courageous and friendly young men,
City of hurried and sparkling waters! City of spires and masts!
City nested in bays! My city!

What Do You Think?

1. Contrast Whitman's view with that of Jefferson. In what ways are they similar? Different? With whom would you agree? Explain.

2. Try to write a poem about your city or the city nearest you. If you can't write a poem, describe that city in several paragraphs.

---

3. Pity the Poor Country Girl*

Theodore Dreiser didn't trust the city any more than did Jefferson. Would a girl who moves to the city today face similar problems to those of Carrie?

*Excerpted from Theodore Dreiser, *Sister Carrie* (1912). New York: Bantam Books.

When Caroline Meeber boarded the afternoon train for Chicago, her total outfit consisted of a small trunk, a cheap imitation alligator-skin satchel, a small lunch in a paper box, and a yellow leather snap purse, containing her ticket, a scrap of paper with her sister's address in VanBuren Street, and four dollars in money. It was August, 1889. She was eighteen years of age, bright, timid, and full of the illusions of ignorance and youth. Whatever touch of regret at parting characterized her thoughts, it was certainly not for advantages now being given up. A gush of tears at her mother's farewell kiss, a touch in her throat when the cars clacked by the flour mill where her father worked by the day, a pathetic sigh as the familiar green environs of the village passed in review, and the threads which bound her so lightly to girlhood and home were irretrievably broken.

To be sure there was always the next station, where one might descend and return. There was the great city, bound more closely by these very trains which came up daily. Columbia City was not so very far away, even once she was in Chicago. What, pray, is a few hours—a few hundred miles? She looked at the little slip bearing her sister's address and wondered. She gazed at the green landscape, now passing in swift review, until her swifter thoughts replaced its impression with vague conjectures of what Chicago might be.

When a girl leaves her home at eighteen, she does one of two things. Either she falls into saving hands and becomes better, or she rapidly assumes the cosmopolitan standard of virtue and becomes worse. Of an intermediate balance, under the circumstances, there is no possibility. The city has its cunning wiles, no less than the infinitely smaller and more human tempter.

There are large forces which allure with all the soulfulness of expression possible in the most cultured human. The gleam of a thousand lights is often as effective as the persuasive light in a wooing and fascinating eye. Half the undoing of the unsophisticated and natural mind is accomplished by forces wholly superhuman. A blare of sound, a roar of life, a vast array of human hives, appeal to the astonished senses in equivocal terms. Without a counsellor at hand to whisper cautious interpretations, what falsehoods may not these things breathe into the unguarded ear? Unrecognized for what they are, their beauty, like music, too often relaxes, then weakens, then perverts the simpler human perceptions.

What Do You Think? _____

From this short excerpt, what would you expect to be the future of Carrie Meeber in the big city? Explain.

4. Are We Our Brother's Keeper?*

Liverpool is not an American city, but the American writer Herman Melville felt moved to describe his experiences there. Similar conditions existed in some American cities in the mid-19th Century. Do conditions like these exist today anywhere? How could you find out?

In going to our boarding-house, the Sign of the Baltimore Clipper, I generally passed through a narrow street called "Launcelott's-Hey," lined with dingy, prison-like cotton warehouses. In this street, or rather alley, you seldom see any one but a truckman, or some solitary old warehousekeeper, haunting his smoky den like a ghost.

Once, passing through this place, I heard a feeble wail, which seemed to come out of the earth. It was but a strip of crooked side-walk where I stood; the dingy wall was on every side, converting the mid-day into twilight; and not a soul was in sight. I started, and could almost have run, when I heard that dismal sound. At last I advanced to an opening which communicated downward with deep tiers of cellars beneath a crumbling old warehouse; and there, some fifteen feet below the walk, crouching in the nameless squalor, with her head bowed over, the figure of what had been a woman. Her blue arms folded to her living bosom two shrunken things like children, that leaned toward her, one on each side. At first, I knew not whether they were alive or dead. They made no sign; they did not move or stir; but from the vault came the soul-sickening wail.

I made a noise with my foot, which, in the silence, echoed far and near; but there was no response. Louder still, when one of the children lifted its head, and cast upward a faint glance; then closed its eyes, and lay motionless. The woman also, now glazed up, and perceived me; but let fall her eye again. They were dumb and next to dead with want. How they had crawled into that den, I could not tell; but there they had crawled to die. At that moment I never thought of relieving them; for death was so stamped in their glazed and unimploring eyes, that I almost regarded them as already no more. I stood looking down on them, while my whole soul swelled within me; and I asked myself, What right had any body in the wide world to smile, and be glad, when sights like this were to be seen? . . .

At last, I walked on toward an open lot in the alley, hoping to meet there some ragged old women, whom I had daily noticed groping amid foul rubbish for little particles of dirty cotton, which they washed out and sold for a trifle.

I found them; and accosting one, I asked if she knew of the persons I had just left. She replied, that she did not; nor did she want to; I then asked another,

*Excerpted from Herman Melville, "The Shame of Liverpool," from *Redburn* (1859).

a miserable, toothless old woman, with a tattered strip of coarse baling stuff round her body. Looking at me for an instant, she resumed her raking in the rubbish, and said that she knew who it was that I spoke of; but that she had no time to attend to beggars and their brats. Accosting still another, who seemed to know my errand, I asked if there was no place to which the woman could be taken. "Yes," she replied, "to the church-yard." I said she was alive, and not dead.

"Then she'll never die," was the rejoinder. "She's been down there these three days with nothing to eat; that I know myself." . . .

Leaving Launcelott's-Hey, I turned into a more frequented street; and soon meeting a policeman, told him of the condition of the woman and the girls.

"It's none of my business, Jack," said he. "I don't belong to that street." Who does, then?"

"I don't know. But what business is it of yours? Are you not a Yankee?"

"Yes," said I, "but come, I will help you remove that woman, if you say so."

"There, now, Jack, go on board your ship and stick to it; leave these matters to the town."

I accosted two more policemen, but with no better success; they would not even go with me to the place. The truth was, it was out of the way, in a silent, secluded spot; and the misery of the three outcasts, hiding away in the ground, did not obtrude upon any one.

Returning to them, I again stamped to attract their attention; but this time none of the three looked up, or even stirred. While I yet stood irresolute, a voice called to me from a high, iron-shuttered window in a loft over the way; and asked what I was about. I beckoned to the man, a sort of porter, to come down, which he did; when I pointed down into the vault.

"Well," said he, "what of it?"

"Can't we get them out?" said I, "haven't you some place in your warehouse where you can put them? Have you nothing for them to eat?"

"You're crazy, boy," said he; "do you suppose that Parkins and Wood want their warehouse turned into a hospital?"

I then went to my boarding-house, and told Handsome Mary of what I had seen; asking her if she could not do something to get the woman and girls removed; or if she could not do that, let me have some food for them. But though a kind person in the main, Mary replied that she gave away enough to beggars in her own street (which was true enough) without looking after the whole neighborhood.

Going into the kitchen, I accosted the cook, a little shriveled-up old Welshwoman with a saucy tongue, whom the sailors called Brandy-Nan; and begged her to give me some cold victuals, if she had nothing better, to take to the vault. But she broke out in a storm of swearing at the miserable occupants of the vault, and refused. I then stepped into the room where our dinner was being spread; and waiting till the girl had gone out, I snatched some

bread and cheese from a stand, and thrusting it into the bosom of my frock, left the house. Hurrying to the lane, I dropped the food down into the vault. One of the girls caught at it convulsively, but fell back, apparently fainting; the sister pushed the other's arm aside, and took the bread in her hand; but with a weak uncertain grasp like an infant's. She placed it to her mouth; but letting it fall again, murmuring faintly something like "water." The woman did not stir; her head was bowed over, just as I had first seen her.

Seeing how it was, I ran down toward the docks to a mean little sailor tavern, and begged for a pitcher; but the cross old man who kept it refused, unless I would pay for it. But I had no money. So as my boarding-house was some way off, and it would be lost time to run to the ship for my big iron pot; under the impulse of the moment, I hurried to one of the Boodle Hydrants, which I remembered having seen running near the scene of a still smoldering fire in an old rag house; and taking off a new tarpaulin hat, which had been loaned me that day, filled it with water.

With this, I returned to Launcelott's-Hey; and with considerable diffi- culty, like getting down into a well, I contrived to descend with it into the vault; where there was hardly enough space left to let me stand. The two girls drank out of the hat together; looking up at me with an unalterable, idiotic expression, that almost made me faint. The woman spoke not a word, and did not stir. . . .

I crawled up into the street, and looking down on them again, almost **13** repented that I had brought them any food; for it would only tend to prolong their misery, without hope of any permanent relief, for die they must very soon; they were too far gone for any medicine to help them. I hardly know whether I ought to confess another thing that occurred to me as I stood there; but it was this—I felt an almost terrible impulse to do them the last mercy, of in some way putting an end to their horrible lives; and I should almost have done so, I think, had I not been deterred by thoughts of the law. For I well knew that the law, which would let them perish of themselves without giving them one cup of water, would spend a thousand pounds, if necessary, in convicting him who should do so much as offer to relieve them from their miserable existence. . . .

I could do no more . . . being obliged to repair to the ship; but at twelve o'clock, when I went to dinner, I hurried into Lancelott's-Hey, when I found that the vault was empty. In place of the woman and children, a heap of quick-lime was glistening. I could not learn who had taken them away, or whither they had gone; but my prayer was answered—they were dead, departed, and at peace.

But again I looked down into the vault, and in fancy beheld the pale, shrunken forms still crouching there. Ah! what are our creeds, and how do we hope to be saved? Tell me, oh Bible, that story of Lazarus again that I may find comfort in my heart for the poor and forlorn. Surrounded as we are by the wants and woes of our fellow-men, and yet given to follow our own pleasures, regardless of their pains, are we not like people sitting up with a corpse, and making merry in the house of the dead?

What Do You Think ⸺⸺⸺⸺⸺⸺⸺⸺⸺⸺⸺⸺⸺⸺

Reread the final paragraph. What is your reaction to that paragraph? Does it hold true for us today? Explain.

---

5. Is Human Behavior the Problem?*

Former head of the U.S. Department of Housing and Urban Development Robert Weaver suggests that the crucial element in the problems of the city is human behavior. Would you agree?

*Abridged from *The Urban Complex* by Robert C. Weaver. Copyright © 1955, 1959 by Atlanta University; Copyright © 1960 by the Academy of Political Science; Copyright © 1964 by Wayne State University; Copyright © 1960, 1961, 1963, 1964 by Robert C. Weaver. Used by permission of Doubleday & Co., Inc.

Cities have always been threatened. A few, like Pompeii, have been wiped out by natural forces. Others have suffered from destruction by man. Human enemies from without and dissension and revolution from within have frequently destroyed or captured and transformed them. They have always been harassed by social problems. For centuries some men have considered cities as centers of evil and sought to destroy this symbol. More recently, we have been told that many urban residents develop guilt feelings about their association with cities. Thus, the recent escape to suburbia may have deep historical and psychological roots. Be that as it may, when technology perfected means of mass transportation, man was able to participate in the city's economic activities at the same time that he centered his family life beyond its borders. Once this occurred, a new concept of urban life, a central city with surburban satellites, developed. The metropolitan area became a reality, and with its rise there appeared a new cluster of urban problems.

In all of the city's problems, the key element has been human beings. People conceived and developed cities. People have constantly threatened them. People, congregating into urban centers, made them the complex social organism we contemplate when the word city is used. It is human beings who, today, are shaping the vast metropolitan areas which house some two-thirds of the population in this Nation. Consequently, it is in terms of people that urban problems must be conceived and their solutions developed.

What Do You Think? _____

1. Weaver states that "it is in terms of people that urban problems must be conceived and their solutions developed." Would you agree or disagree? Give your reasons.

2. What reasons for the growth of suburban living does Weaver give? Do you agree or disagree with him? Why?

_____

6. City Life: Enrichment or Existence?*

In recent years people have come to be more concerned than in the past about the kind of life that can be lived in the cities. What hope does the article below hold out for urban life?

*"Urban Environment: Cities Made for People," *Senior Scholastic,* February 8, 1971. Copyright © 1971 by Scholastic Magazines, Inc.

> Communities should be planned with an eye to the effect made upon the human spirit by being continually surrounded with a maximum of beauty.
>
> Thomas Jefferson

> Caution: Cities May be Hazardous to Your Health.
>
> Students at Adams High School
> Portland, Oregon

Something happened in America between the time Jefferson wrote about "planned communities" in the early 19th century and the warning issued last year by the Adams students. What happened was the growth of the American city, unplanned and uncontrolled.

Today seven out of every ten Americans live in cities. In the past 15 years, more than 12 million people have moved from rural areas into cities. The U.S. Census Bureau estimates that another one hundred million people will be added to our present population by the end of this century. Nearly all of them are expected to live in or near cities.

What kind of life will they have? Will it be different from life in the city now?

The list of urban ills is long and well known today. The environmental problems which exist everywhere often seem so much greater in the city: air pollution, noise, garbage, overcrowding.

During the 1950's and 1960's vast programs were undertaken to improve life in the cities. While there were some successes, many people believe that these programs often only intensified the problems they were designed to solve.

Let's look at just two examples: housing and highways. A lot of slums were torn down, but many of the public housing projects which replaced them were no better. They quickly became "high-rise" slums. The Pruitt-Igoe housing complex in St. Louis, now 15 years old, is a startling example.

The 43 buildings in this massive project (26 are now boarded up and vacant) just aggravated the evils they were supposed to eliminate. Crime and vandalism became serious problems, the buildings deteriorated rapidly. The people there were not consulted in the planning, and there has never been any sense of community. The project, it is generally agreed now, has been a "monumental failure."[1]

Highways built to relieve traffic congestion often have just the opposite effect. By encouraging more people to drive into the cities, they increase the congestion and the air pollution in the city center.

Highways often eat up the best land in and near the city. They run over valuable park land or along waterfronts. Highway planners, looking for the least expensive route, frequently slice through established neighborhoods, disrupting the lives of many people.

While new expressways are built, mass transit systems in most cities are allowed to decay. Fares go up, and service goes down.

16　　[1] *Ed. note:* Some of the buildings have been destroyed by the housing authority. See Chapter 6.

The zoning laws in most metropolitan areas encourage use of the automobile, too. Areas are usually designated for one use only: residential, commercial, industrial, etc. A suburbanite often must have a car just to go to the movies or to buy a loaf of bread.

Lewis Mumford, author of *The City in History,* says: "The first lesson we have to learn is that a city exists, not for the constant passage of motorcars, but for the care and culture of men."

"The care and culture of men." That means cities for people. And that quality, say many of the experts, is just what is missing in cities today. Neighborhoods are torn apart, buildings go up—often without concern for the people directly involved.

Is it possible to create an urban environment in which the human spirit will be "continually surrounded with a maximum of beauty," as Thomas Jefferson wished? Most architects and city planners answer "yes" but they disagree on the approach. Some would build whole new cities from scratch. Others would try to improve the quality of life in our existing cities.

Athelstan Spilhaus, a city planner and designer of experimental cities, would build whole new cities in which all utilities and vehicles that might pollute the air would go underground. They would be scattered evenly across the U.S. Each city would be completely planned in advance and limited in size. Frank L. Hope, Jr., head of a San Diego architectural and planning firm, envisions an "Earth City" of 2 ½ million people built from scratch in "the spacious interior of our continent."

On a less grand scale, several "new towns" are already being built in the U.S. An example is Columbia, Md., midway between Baltimore and Washington, D.C. When finished in 1980, it will house 110,000 people and provide jobs for 30,000.

Among the principles governing the design of the new towns are these: plenty of open space, essential services within walking distance, and a good public transportation system.

But there are many others who oppose the "new city" idea. Wolf Von Eckardt, architecture critic of the Washington Post, calls them "cop-out cities." He says they only "evade the task of cleaning up the mess we have made of urban America."

Architect Nathaniel A. Owings says that all natural locations for cities have already been used. "Satellite cities and new towns are unnatural and should not be encouraged," he says. "We can organize our old cities so that they become comfortable places for man to work and to live."

How? By making the pedestrian the center of all plans, says Lewis Mumford. "Nothing would do more to give life back to our blighted urban cores than to reinstate the pedestrian," he says. Give man pleasant places to walk, Mumford urges, and scrap the zoning laws so that things he needs are within walking distance.

Improvement of urban life should be a major priority of the federal government, says Donald Alexander, counsel for the National League of

Cities. That means developing and implementing a national urban policy. Alexander's scheme would "coordinate transportation, housing, industry, and other public facility development in one closely knit growth plan which features the needs of individual citizens."

In many instances, the push for a better urban environment has come from individual citizens or community and neighborhood groups. Begun on a small scale, their actions often have wider effects. Take Redondo Beach, Calif., for example. A community organization planted some trees along one shopping street. Soon the merchants began to sweep their sidewalks more frequently. And it wasn't long before several of the storefronts underwent faceliftings.

Young people who live in cities are taking steps to improve the urban environment, too. Students at Stuyvesant High School in New York City helped clean up a vacant lot and turn it into a playground. Teens in Newark, N.J., donned candy-striped coats and stood on street corners urging passersby not to litter. They are all trying to stop the decay of our cities, trying to answer this statement by the students at Portland's Adams High:

"By the year 2000, 85 per cent of the American people will live in cities. That is, they will be located in cities, but whether the cities will not be buried in garbage, whether there will be enough unpolluted air and water, whether the level of noise will be tolerable—whether life and not just existence is possible—remain serious and unanswered questions."

What Do You Think?

1. "The people were not consulted in the planning." Is it important for people to have a voice in planning their living environment? How can this be done?
2. What actions can you or your class take which would make your environment more human and livable?

7. Another View of City Problems*

Some people maintain that the big city has outgrown its usefulness and that the solution lies in smaller units. In the biggest of the big cities, New York, the problem facing the mayor have prompted the question of whether it is possible to govern a city of this size. Here are some of former Mayor John Lindsay's views near the start of his term as mayor.

Our cities exact too much from those who live in them. They are not only increasingly expensive places in which to live or work; more and more, the price of city living is being paid by a sacrifice of fundamental personal freedoms.

*Excerpted from John V. Lindsay, "The Future of the American City," *Saturday Review,* January 1966. Copyright © 1966 by Saturday Review, Inc.

Freedom to use the sidewalks and parks at night without fear.

Freedom to rent an apartment or buy a house at a reasonable cost.

Freedom to send children to school with the knowledge the classrooms will be bright and clean, the teachers skilled, and the instruction challenging.

Freedom to find a job or join a union without being frustrated by racial or religious discrimination.

Freedom to move about the city with reasonable speed and convenience on a public transportation system.

Freedom to breathe the air and use the waterways with equanimity.

City residents must, of course, adjust to some impositions to gain the varied advantages of urban living. Crowds, noise and rush, for example, are natural components of the city's pervasive excitement. But most of our major cities offer more liabilities than attractions. They have not succeeded in providing environments that meet ordinary standards of pleasure and comfort because they have not learned how to cope with the basic urban problems that vitiate our amenities and our liberties. The failure, however, is not uniform; every American city can learn from the individual successes of others.

Chicago, for example, reduced its crime rate for two consecutive years by tripling the number of patrol cars, speeding up communications, and eliminating redundant paperwork.

Pittsburgh marshaled its business community to overcome its once legendary air pollution problem. Los Angeles took extraordinary but practical steps to ensure its water supply. Philadelphia has led in rehabilitation slum housing, St. Louis in waterfront development, and San Francisco in the planning of a unified, area transportation system.

The specific routes to these accomplishments cannot always be followed by other cities. But they deserve rigorous inspection and evaluation. . . .

The real barriers to the workable, enjoyable city, however, are frustration, despair and cynicism. I believe they can be surmounted by creating a city government created by staffing City Hall with the finest talent, the most dedicated professionals, and the keenest minds, without obeisance to party affiliations. Cities should abandon the petty self-defeating practice of trying to operate with an officialdom expediently drawn from relatives, precinct captains, special interest groups, campaign contributors and party hacks. The invariably tragic result is to render it impossible to attract into city government the men and women of excellence the city vitally needs; they may scarifice top salaries and normal hours to serve their city, but they will not relinquish their pride to an administration with a vision curtailed by the next election date. **19**

It is not enough, however, to rest on the basically inner-directed concept of attracting the best administrators. City Hall must extend itself to the residents of the city whose only personal contact with their government often takes the form of a policeman, a housing inspector, or an ambulance driver. The widespread estrangement—often a pronounced alienation—that characterizes the relationship between a city government and its citizens can be bridged by granting people a strong, direct voice in the affairs of their city. Mayors might explore the establishment of neighborhood offices throughout their cities to give residents a line into City Hall when they want answers or action on such perennial problems as better street lights, smoke abatement, vandalism, landlord-tenant disputes, and enforcement of dog leash laws. The immediate objective would be to obtain results on sensible requests and justifiable complaints. . . .

These will be adventurous years in American cities, for in their span we shall do much to decide whether major cities will rise proudly at the center of disintegrate at the core of our intensely populated and still expanding urban complexes. The outcome will be crucially important, for the issue in the struggle to achieve livable cities is not only the nature of our increasingly urban society, but the nature of our future civilization.

What Do You Think? _____

1. Lindsay lists six freedoms which city dwellers give up as a price for living in the city. Is this true in your city? Is city living worth such a price? Explain your reasoning.

2. What are your feelings about your local government? Is it effective? Is it representative of you and your family? If not, how could it be made more so?

---

8. A New Mayor Responds to the Urban Crisis*

In 1974 the voters of Detroit selected Coleman Young as their mayor. Mr. Young was the first black mayor of Detroit. He is one of an increasing number of black people to be elected to head major city governments. In his inaugural address, he identifies several priorities for his administration. Does your city have any of the problems spotlighted by Mayor Young?

*Inaugural address of Mayor Coleman A. Young, January 2, 1974.

. . . The first problem that we must face as citizens of this great city—the first fact that we must look squarely in the eye—is that this city has too long been polarized. We can no longer afford the luxury of hatred and racial division. What is good for the black people of this city is good for the white people of this city. What is good for the rich people of this city is good for the poor people in this city. What is good for those who live in the suburbs is good for those of us who live in the central city.

It is clear that we have a commonality of interest. The suburb cannot live without the city. The white population of this city cannot live while its black people suffer discrimination and poverty.

And so I dedicate myself, with the help of the Common Council, and more basically with your help, toward beginning now to attack the economic deterioration of our city—to move forward. The significant first steps have been made at the Renaissance Center to deal with the problem of rebuilding our city economically. And I recognize the economic problem as a basic one, but there is also a problem of crime, which is not unrelated to poverty and unemployment, and so I say we must attack both of these problems vigorously at the same time.

The police department alone cannot rid this city of crime. The police must have the respect and cooperation of our citizens. But they must earn that respect by extending our citizens cooperation and respect. We must build a new people-oriented police department and then you and they can help us to drive the criminals from our streets.

I issue an open warning now to all dope pushers, to all rip-off artists, to all muggers: It's time to leave Detroit. Hit Eight Mile Road. And I don't give a damn if they are black or white, if they wear super fly suits or blue uniforms with silver badges. HIT THE ROAD.

With your help we shall move forward to a new and greater Detroit. We must first believe in ourselves. We must first do for ourselves. Yes, we will demand our share of revenues from Washington and from Lansing. But the job begins here and now—with us.

Ladies and gentlemen, the time for rhetoric[1] is past. The time for working is here. The time for moving ahead is upon us. Let's move forward together.

What Do You Think? _____

1. What does Mayor Young see as the most important problem for his city?
2. Do city dwellers have a "commonality of interest"? What does this mean?
3. Mayor Young states that the police alone cannot rid a city of crime. What does he mean? Who else must help?

---

[1]Showy language.

9. The City Needs Help

Or so says this cartoonist. Would you agree?

"HELP!"

Photoreporters, Inc. from *The Herblock Gallery* (Simon & Schuster, 1968).

This cartoon was drawn in 1966. How have conditions in cities changed since then—or have they?

ACTIVITIES FOR INVOLVEMENT

1. As the chapter points out, there are many different ways of looking at the city. Historically we have viewed it as both a "slough of despond" and a great center of opportunity. Arrange a debate among members of the class on the question, Resolved: That the American city is the hope of our future.

2. Form a small committee to arrange a visit to City Hall. It would be wise to arrange in advance for interviews with those people you wish to see. Attempt to find out the answer to the question: Is it possible to govern this city? If you find that the answer you are given, or the answer that you personally arrive at, is "no," attempt to create a new plan for government or a new form of living arrangement other than the city. Present your paper to the class for discussion.

3. People and their habits are a large part of the city's problem. Make a list of habits that make the city a good place to live, and a contrasting list of habits that make it an unpleasant place. How could you change some of the harmful habits?

4. Write your own view of your city. Let your imagination go and attempt to capture whatever it is that makes your city an exciting and dynamic place. If you find it otherwise, try to capture this also.

5. Listed below are a number of words that writers have used to describe the city. Which do you think are most appropriate? Least? Why?

exciting	dying	dirty
ugly	moving	golden
sick	warm	turbulent
electric	alive	hard
vibrant	cold	frightening

    What words would you add to the list? How would you describe the city in a few sentences?

3
SLUMS AND SUBURBS: TWO NATIONS—DIVISIBLE

Every large city in the United States has its slums—sections of older, deteriorating housing. And there are rural slums, too. These are the shantytowns, often populated by migrant farm workers or others who have been cut off from the affluence that characterizes middle-class life in America.

In the cities, slums are caused by many factors. Increasing age of buildings, failure on the part of landowners to keep up their property, the desire for maximum profit which impels landlords to subdivide homes into apartments, the processes of racial discrimination which force black people to live in ghettos owned by whites who care little for the nature of the community they are helping to create—all help to cause our slums.

Providing adequate housing for the nation has been an issue in this country for a long time. In 1939, Congress passed the Federal Housing Authority Act, which provided a federal guarantee for mortgages. The G.I. Bill of Rights in World War II provided for low-interest loans to veterans of the war. Korean and Vietnam veterans also earned such rights. Immense amounts of housing have been built since the war to accommodate the increased population. But most of this housing has been built in suburban areas, and little of it has gone to the poor. Only 650,000 units of federally sponsored public housing have been built in the nation. Urban renewal programs aimed at destroying the slums have earned the nickname "Negro removal," for often low-priced housing has been replaced with middle-and upper-priced housing which the people who lived in the area before the renewal cannot afford.

In 1968 Congress passed a new housing bill aimed at remedying some of these ills. This act has not been effective and people continue to live under conditions such as those described in the readings that follow.

1. Slums Are Not New to Our Nation*

The fight against our slums has been a long one and, as the following reading shows, people in the past have thought the battle was won. How would you respond to this author?

*Excerpted from Jacob A. Riis, "The Battle with the Slum," *Jubilee—One Hundred Years of the Atlantic* (Boston: Little, Brown & Co., 1957).

The slum complaint had been chronic in all ages, but the great changes which the nineteenth century saw, the new industry, political freedom, brought on an acute attack which threatened to become fatal. Too many of us had supposed that, built as our commonwealth was on universal suffrage, it would be proof against the complaints that harassed older states; but in fact it turned out that there was extra hazard in that. Having solemnly resolved that all men are created equal and have certain inalienable rights, among them life, liberty, and the pursuit of happiness, we shut our eyes and waited for the formula to work. . . .

So the battle began. . . . [T]he civic conscience awoke in 1879.

In that year the slum was arraigned in the churches. The sad and shameful story was told of how it grew and was fostered by avarice that saw in the homeless crowds from over the sea only a chance for business and exploited them to the uttermost, making sometimes a hundred per cent on the capital invested—always most out of the worst houses, from the tenants of which "nothing was expected" save that they pay the usurious rents—how Christianity, citizenship, human fellowship, shook their skirts clear of the rabble that was only good enough to fill the greedy purse, and how the rabble, left to itself, improved such opportunities as it found after such fashion as it knew; how it ran elections merely to count its thugs in, and fattened at the public crib; and how the whole evil thing had its root in the tenements, where the home had ceased to be sacred—those dark and deadly dens in which the family ideal was tortured to death and character was smothered, in which children were "damned rather than born" into the world, thus realizing a slum kind of foreordination to torment, happily brief in many cases. The Tenement House Committee long afterward called the worst of the barracks "infant slaughterhouses," and showed, by reference to the mortality lists, that they killed one in every five babies born in them.

The story shocked the town into action. Plans for a better kind of tenement were called for, and a premium was put on every ray of light and breath of air that could be let into it. Money was raised to build model houses, and a bill to give the health authorities summary powers in dealing with tenements was sent to the legislature. The landlords held it up until the last day of the session, when it was forced through by an angered public opinion. The power of the cabal was broken. The landlords had found their Waterloo. Many of them got rid of their property, which in a large number of cases they had never seen, and tried to forget the source of their ill-gotten wealth. Light and air did find their way into the tenements in a halfhearted fashion, and we began to count the tenants as "souls." That is one of our milestones in the history of New York. They were never reckoned so before; no one ever thought of them as "souls." So, restored to human fellowship, in the twilight of the air shaft that had penetrated to their dens, the first Tenement House Committee was able to make them out "better than the houses" they lived in, and a long step forward was taken. The Mulberry Bend, the wicked core of the "bloody Sixth Ward," was marked for destruction, and all slumdom held its breath to see it go. With that gone, it seemed as if the old days must be gone too, never to return. . . .

The streets are cleaned; the slum has been washed. Even while I am writing, a bill is urged in the legislature to build in every senatorial district in the city a gymnasium and a public bath. It matters little whether it passes at this session or not. The important thing is that it is there. The rest will follow. A people's club is being organized to crowd out the saloon that has had a monopoly of the brightness and the cheer in the tenement streets too long. The labor unions are bestirring themselves to deal with the sweating curse, and the gospel of less law and more enforcement sits enthroned at Albany. Theodore Roosevelt will teach us again Jefferson's forgotten lesson, that "the whole art of government consists in being honest."

One after another, the outworks of the slum have been taken. The higher standards now set up on every hand, in the cleaner streets, in the better schools, in the parks and the clubs, in the settlements, and in the thousand and one agencies for good that touch and help the lives of the poor at as many points, will tell at no distant day and react upon the homes and upon their builders. Philanthropy is not sitting idle and waiting. It is building tenements on the human plan that lets in sunshine and air and hope. It is putting up hotels deserving of the name for the army that just now had no other home than the cheap lodging houses which Inspector Byrnes firmly called "nurseries of crime." These are standards from which there is no backing down, and they are here to stay, for they pay. That is the test. Not charity, but justice—that is the gospel which they preach.

What Do You Think? _____

1. Mr. Riis is very optimistic in his conclusion, written before the twentieth century had begun. Write a letter to Mr. Riis in which you point out to him how his dreams have been realized or how the city has failed to live up to his expectations.

2. The author thinks that dealing with the slum is a matter of justice. What does he mean by this? What type of justice is he talking about?

3. Do you think there would be the same kind of opposition today to clearing up the slums that there was in the late nineteenth century? Defend your position on this question.

2. What It's Like in the Alley*

Psychiatrist Robert Coles has for many years written of the struggles of the poor, particularly poor children, to survive. The following selections include comments of a mother and son who have come from the South to Boston. How do the conditions described compare with conditions where you live?

*Robert Coles, "What It's Like in the Alley," *Daedalus,* Fall 1968.

"In the alley it's mostly dark, even if the sun is out. But if you look around, you can find things. I know how to get into every building except that it's like night once you're inside them, because they don't have lights. So, I stay here. You're better off. It's no good on the street. You can get hurt all the time, one way or the other. And in buildings, like I told you, it's bad in them, too. But here it's o.k. You can find your own corner, and if someone tries to move in you fight him off. We meet here all the time, and figure out what we'll do next. It might be a game, or over for some pool, or a coke or something. You need to have a place to start out from, and that's like it is in the alley; you can always know your buddy will be there, provided it's the right time. So you go there, and you're on your way, man."

Like all children of nine, Peter is always on his way—to a person, a place, a "thing" he wants to do. "There's this here thing we thought we'd try tomorrow," he'll say; and eventually I'll find out that he means there's to be a race. He and his friends will compete with another gang to see who can wash a car faster and better. The cars belong to four youths who make their money taking bets, and selling liquor that I don't believe was ever purchased, and pushing a few of those pills that "go classy with beer."

Peter lives in the heart of what we in contemporary America have chosen (ironically, so far as history goes) to call an "urban ghetto." The area was a slum before it became a ghetto, and there still are some very poor white people on its edges and increasing numbers of Puerto Ricans in several of its blocks. Peter was not born in the ghetto, nor was his family told to go there. They are Americans and have been here "since way back before anyone can remember." That is the way Peter's mother talks about Alabama, about the length of time she and her ancestors have lived there. She and Peter's father came north "for freedom." They did not seek out a ghetto, an old quarter of Boston

where they were expected to live and where they would be confined, yet at least some of the time solidly at rest, with kin, and reasonably safe.

* * * * *

What is "life" like for her over there, where she lives, in the neighborhood she refers to as "here"?

"When I go to bed at night I tell myself I've done good, to stay alive and keep the kids alive, and if they'll just wake up in the morning, and me too, well then, we can worry about that, all the rest, come tomorrow. So there you go. We do our best, and that's all you can do."

* * * * *

When I first met Peter and his mother, I wanted to know how they lived, what they did with their time, what they liked to do or disliked doing, what they believed. I cannot think of a better way to begin knowing what life is like for Peter and his mother than to hear the following and hear it again and think about its implications: "No sir, Peter has never been to a doctor, not unless you count the one at school, and she's a nurse I believe. He was his sickest back home before we came here, and you know there was no doctor for us in the county. In Alabama you have to pay a white doctor first, before he'll go near you. And we don't have but a few colored ones. (I've never seen a one.) There was this woman we'd go to, and she had gotten some nursing education in Mobile. (No, I don't know if she was a nurse or not, or a helper to the nurses, maybe.) Well, she would come to help us. With the convulsions, she'd show you how to hold the child, and make sure he doesn't hurt himself. They can bite their tongues real, real bad.

"Here, I don't know what to do. There's the city hospital, but it's no good for us. I went there with my husband, no sooner than a month or so after we came up here. We waited and waited, and finally the day was almost over. We left the kids with a neighbor, and we barely knew her. I said it would take the morning, but I never thought we'd get home near suppertime. And they wanted us to come back and come back, because it was something they couldn't do all at once—though for most of the time we just sat there and did nothing. And my husband, he said his stomach was the worse for going there, and he'd take care of himself from now on, rather than go there.

"Maybe they could have saved him. But they're far away, and I didn't have money to get a cab, even if there was one around here, and I thought to myself it'll make him worse, to take him there.

"My kids, they get sick. The welfare worker, she sends a nurse here, and she tells me we should be on vitamins and the kids need all kinds of check-ups. Once she took my daughter and told her she had to have her teeth looked at, and the same with Peter. So, I went with my daughter, and they didn't see me that day, but said they could in a couple of weeks. And I had to pay the woman next door to mind the little ones, and there was the carfare, and we sat and sat, like before. So, I figured, it would take more than we've got to see that dentist. And when the nurse told us we'd have to come back a few times— **29** that's how many, a few—I thought that no one ever looked at my teeth, and they're not good, I'll admit, but you can't have everything, that's what I say, and that's what my kids have to know, I guess."

* * * * *

(Peter) ". . . I go to school. I eat what I can and leave. I have two changes of clothes, one for everyday and one for Sunday. I wait on my friend Billy, and we're off by 8:15. He's from around here, and he's a year older. He knows everything. He can tell you if a woman is high on some stuff, or if she's been drinking, or she's off her mind about something. He knows. His brother has a convertible, a Buick. He pays off the police, but Billy won't say no more than that.

"In school we waste time until it's over. I do what I have to. I don't like the place. I feel like falling off all day, just putting my head down and saying good-bye to everyone until three. We're out then, and we sure wake up. I don't have to stop home first, not now. I go with Billy. We'll be in the alley, or we'll go to see them play pool. Then you know when it's time to go home. You hear someone say six o'clock, and you go in. I eat and I watch television. It must be around ten or eleven I'm in bed."

Peter sees rats all the time. He has been bitten by them. He has a big stick by his bed to use against them. They also claim the alley, even in the daytime. They are not large enough to be compared with cats, as some observers have insisted; they are simply large, confident, well-fed, unafraid rats. The garbage is theirs; the land is theirs, the tenement is theirs; human flesh is theirs. When I first started visiting Peter's family, I wondered why they didn't do something to rid themselves of those rats, and the cockroaches, and the mosquitoes, and the flies, and the maggots, and the ants, and especially the garbage in the alley which attracts so much of all that "lower life." Eventually I began to see some of the reasons why. A large apartment building with many families has exactly two barrels in its basement. The halls of the building go unlighted. Many windows have no screens, and some windows are broken and boarded up. The stairs are dangerous; some of them missing timber ("We just jump over them," says Peter cheerfully.) And the landowner is no one in particular. Rent is collected by an agent, in the name of a "realty trust." Somewhere in City Hall there is a bureaucrat who unquestionably might be persuaded to prod someone in the "trust"; and one day I went with three of the tenants, including Peter's mother, to try that "approach." We waited and waited at City Hall. (I drove us there, clear across town, naturally.) Finally we met up with a man, a not very encouraging or inspiring or generous or friendly man. He told us we would have to try yet another department and swear out a complaint; and that the "case" would have to be "studied," and that we would then be "notified of a decision." We went to the department down the hall, and waited some more, another hour and ten minutes. By then it was three o'clock, and the mothers wanted to go home. They weren't thinking of rats anymore, or poorly heated apartments, or garbage that had nowhere to go and often went uncollected for two weeks, not one. They were thinking of their children, who would be home from school and, in the case of two women, their husbands who would also soon be home. "Maybe we should come back some other day."

* * * * *

... His teacher may not know it, but Peter is a good sociologist, and a good political scientist, a good student of urban affairs. With devastating accuracy he can reveal how much of the "score" he knows; yes, and how fearful and sad and angry he is: "This here city isn't for us. It's for the people downtown. We're here because, like my mother said, we had to come. If they could lock us up or sweep us away, they would. That's why I figure the only way you can stay ahead is get some kind of deal for yourself. If I had a choice I'd live someplace else, but I don't know where. It would be a place where they treated you right, and they didn't think you were some nuisance. But the only thing you can do is be careful of yourself; if not, you'll get killed somehow, like it happened to my father."

* * * * *

... It may comfort me to know that every American city provides some free medical services for its "indigent," but Peter's mother and thousands like her have quite a different view of things: "I said to you the other time, I've tried there. It's like at City Hall, you wait and wait, and they pushes you and shove you and call your name, only to tell you to wait some more, and if you tell them you can't stay there all day, they'll say 'lady, go home, then.' You get sick just trying to get there. You have to give your children over to people or take them all with you; and the carfare is expensive. Why if we had a doctor around here, I could almost pay him with the carfare it takes to get there and back for all of us. And you know, they keep on having you come back and back, and they don't know what each other says. Each time they starts from scratch."

It so happens that recently I took Peter to a children's hospital and arranged for a series of evaluations which led to the following: a pair of glasses; a prolonged bout of dental work; antibiotic treatment for skin lesions; a thorough cardiac work-up, with the subsequent diagnosis of rheumatic heart disease; a conference between Peter's mother and a nutritionist, because the boy has been on a high-starch, low-protein and low-vitamin diet all his life. He suffers from one attack of sinus trouble after another, from a succession of sore throats and earaches, from cold upon cold, even in the summer. A running nose is unsurprising to him—and so is chest pain and shortness of breath, due to a heart ailment, we now know.

At the same time Peter is tough. I have to emphasize again how tough. Peter has learned to be wary as well as angry; tentative as well as extravagant; at times controlled and only under certain circumstances defiant: "Most of the time, I think you have to watch your step. That's what I think. That's the difference between up here and down in the South. That's what my mother says, and she's right. Here, you measure the next guy first and then make your move when you think it's a good time to."

He was talking about "how you get along" when you leave school and go "mix with the guys" and start "getting your deal." He was telling me what an outrageous and unsafe world he has inherited and how very carefully he has made his appraisal of the future. Were I afflicted with some of his physical complaints, I would be fretful, annoyed, petulant,[1] angry—and moved to do something, see someone, get a remedy, a pill, a promise of help. He has made his "adjustment" to the body's pain, and he has also learned to contend with the alley and the neighborhood and us, the world beyond: "The cops come by here all the time. They drive up and down the street. They want to make sure everything is o.k. to look at. They don't bother you, so long as you don't get in their way."

What Do You Think?

1. What words would you use to describe Peter's mother? How would you describe the life which she and her family lead?
2. The more money and education people have, the more alternatives they seem to see for their lives. What are Peter's alternatives?
3. It could be said that for Peter school is both no hope and the only hope he has. What does this contradictory statement mean? Would you agree? Why or why not?

3. A Community Is More Than Buildings*

Parts of the South Bronx in New York City were being dramatically changed in 1973. New buildings were taking the place of old, dilapidated structures. But the problems of this area went far beyond new construction

The fire hydrants are open, even in this biting cold weather—town pumps that provide the sole water supply for drinking, washing and sanitation for thousands of tenants in 20 percent of the housing in the area. When one hydrant freezes over, the residents pry open another.

Packs of wild dogs pick through the rubble and roam the streets, sometimes attacking residents. As protection, many mailmen, health workers and deliverers carry dog repellent.

A drug pusher is murdered by a youth gang acting on a $30 contract from a rival pusher. A youngster is nearly stomped to death outside a school in an argument over a soda bottle. Merchants close their stores at sunset even though many are armed and some conduct business inside their stores behind bullet-proof glass.

---

[1]Irritable.
*Martin Tolchin, *The New York Times Service*, "A Community Is More Than Buildings," *San Francisco Chronicle/Examiner,* January 28, 1973.

This is the South Bronx today—violent, drugged, burned out, graffiti-splattered and abandoned.

Forty percent of the 400,000 residents are on welfare, and 30 percent of the employables are unemployed.

Over the last ten years, middle-class whites have fled the South Bronx, which is now home to a young, shifting population that is 65 percent Puerto Rican and other Hispanics and the remainder blacks.

Even for a native New Yorker, the voyage to the South Bronx is a journey to a foreign country where fear is the overriding emotion in a landscape of despair. The residents, who have long been afraid to go out at night, are now afraid to go out during the day into streets menaced by 20,000 drug addicts and 9,500 gang members.

"The South Bronx is . . . a city of death." says Dr. Harold Wise, founder of the Martin Luther King Jr. Health Center at Third Avenue and East 169th Street in the Bathgate section. "There's a total breakdown of services, looting is rampant, fires are everywhere."

A study conducted by the King Health Center last year showed not only that 20 percent of the houses were without water, but also that 50 percent were without heat half the time.

"There's a very rapid deterioration of the body in many people here after the age of 25," Dr. Wise says. "Something happens to your body when you spend the entire winter without heat."

* * * * *

A 37-year-old drug pusher is fatally struck by six bullets that shape a cross on his body. A bus is invaded and its driver held at gunpoint, while passengers are relieved of wallets, watches and other valuables, Wild West style. A runaway girl is crippled after being beaten with belts and chains.

These acts of violence, all committed last month, were among more than 800 reported examples of violent crimes last year that have been linked by police to the youth gangs that have been proliferating in the South Bronx.

Street gangs had terrorized slum areas, including the South Bronx, during the 1950s and the early 1960s. Many experts say these gangs broke up after their members became addicted to heroin and in their drug-induced torpor[1] dropped out. But now, health and community officials in the South Bronx say they have observed a marked increase in youth violence that has accompanied a marked decrease in overdose cases and other indicators of narcotics use.

There are those in the South Bronx who credit the gangs with routing drug pushers and restoring a feeling of pride. But others contend that few gangs are drug-free and that some of them are used by drug dealers as armies to consolidate their power.

Many residents also complain that the gangs have unleashed a reign of terror on their neighbors, menacing merchants, assaulting students in virtually all of the borough's schools and, in some cases, wounding women and children, bystanders caught in the gunplay.

[1]Sluggishness.

All residents, however, feel that the reappearance of the gangs represents an important symptom of the sickness of the South Bronx. To many residents, too many youngsters in their community are faced with only two choices—the walking death of narcotics or the violent world of the street gangs.

* * * * *

The gangs, which call themselves "cliques," say they have 9,500 members, ranging in age from 13 to 30. Most are Puerto Ricans, many are homeless and almost all are estranged from their families. Most gangs are headquartered in abandoned buildings, some of which were vacated after the gangs moved in and set fire to other apartments in search of lebensraum.[2]

To gang members, headquarters is home, a haven against the biting winds, an emotional sustenance against the isolation from society that they feel. Most headquarters are heated by gas ovens with mattresses tossed in disarray on the floor. The black walls are covered with Day-Glo paintings, with violent and obscene themes illuminated by fluorescent lighting.

Why have youths in the South Bronx banded together into gangs?

"They're lost in a maze of nothing out there so they go to a gang looking for status and identity," Sergeant Craig Collins, supervisor of the police department intelligence unit in the Bronx, says.

Gang members themselves offer other reasons for banding together.

"We're a group of guys working together to help out the people," says Ace, the president of the Cypress Bachelors.

Ace is a 17-year-old Puerto Rican who carries himself with hauteur and likes to strut down the street flanked by his two "wives." Like many gang members, Ace is a dropout from Clinton High School. "I wasn't learning anything. I had fights every day," he explains.

Ace stresses that drugs are not tolerated in his club.

Their disdain of heroin has led some gangs to boast that they have driven pushers from their neighborhood streets.

Some community workers have words of praise for the gangs. Carmelo Saez, who works with gangs at the King Health Center, finds "streaks of violence," but also believes "some have done some good."

"They've cleaned up the neighborhoods," he says. "They have chased junkies and pushers out of their blocks."

* * * * *

While politicians parry responsibility, the South Bronx remains home to women on the street who appear to be in their mid-forties or fifties, but who are known to Esther Hunter, a public health nurse, to be in their early twenties. It is home to a seven-year-old wino, swaying before a building on a street corner and to his 12-year-old addict brother, who injects himself with heroin in a "shooting gallery" in the basement of the building.

It is a community where rage always lurks just below the surface and often erupts in acts of seemingly mindless violence. It is a place where a dissenter at a meeting of a Model Cities policy committee was murdered by being dragged into the street and thrown under a moving car.

Rage also takes the form of massive vandalism that further deprives an already disadvantaged community of life's necessities.

The abandoned, burned-out buildings on Fox Street are typical of those throughout the South Bronx. For the last 11 years, Olga Colon, an elderly woman, has lived at 871 Tiffany Street—an abandoned building without heat or water for the last eight months. The building houses a pharmacy and a grocery store.

"I get water from the grocery store," Mrs. Colon says. "When I need a toilet, I go to a friend. I don't pay nothing—no rent—for eight months."

There are 3,000 to 5,000 abandoned buildings in the South Bronx, according to Jorge Battista, former deputy director of the Bronx Model Cities Program who is now deputy borough president.

"I've seen people run a wire from a building with electricity to one without electricity," Battista says. "A very dangerous business."

* * * * *

Yet . . . and Yet: Few devastated areas of New York City show such outward, visible signs of renewal as does the South Bronx. Construction cranes dominate a skyline of one area. The shell of a new 1,000-bed hospital towers above, near two newly completed schools and a 1,530-unit public-housing project that is well under way.

But this public construction—perhaps more than in any other part of the city—is simply not enough to reverse the complicated social and economic pathology of an area in which civilization has virtually disappeared.

35

Moreover, the despair that has accompanied the disintegration of the South Bronx has started to infect the thinking and plans of all levels of government. After a belated and faltering start that made the current building boom possible, city, state and federal agencies now seem to be abandoning much of their efforts to reclaim the South Bronx.

Nobody has the answers.

* * * * *

Two schools of thought have emerged from those familiar with the South Bronx. Some believe that the problems can be solved by massive infusions of government funds and programs.

Others hold that the problems are insoluble, even if the government had the resources. They say that the South Bronx should be leveled and its residents relocated and that never again should the city allow such a concentration of poverty and human need.

What Do You Think? _____

1. The gangs claim they are helping the residents of the South Bronx. Are they? Why or why not?

2. If you were a social planner, what solutions would you advise for the people in the South Bronx?

3. Which of the two schools of thought concerning the South Bronx would you support? Why? What other alternatives can you suggest as to what might be done?

---

4. Ballad of the Landlord*

The black poet Langston Hughes summed up the feelings of many who live in the slums and ghettoes in the brief poem that follows. What are some of the social evils he is attacking in this work?

Landlord, landlord,
My roof has sprung a leak.
Don't you 'member I told you about it
Way last week?

Landlord, landlord,
These steps is broken down.

---

*Langston Hughes, "Ballad of the Landlord," in *Selected Poems of Langston Hughes* (New York: Alfred A. Knopf, 1959).

When you come up yourself
It's a wonder you don't fall down.

Ten Bucks you say I owe you?
Ten Bucks you say is due?
Well, that's Ten Bucks more'n I'll pay you
Till you fix this house up new.

What? You gonna get eviction orders?
You gonna cut off my heat?
You gonna take my furniture and
Throw it in the street?

Um-huh! You talking high and mighty.
Talk on—till you get through
You aint gonna be able to say a word
If I land my fist on you.

Police! Police!
Come and get this man!
He's trying to ruin the government
And overturn the land!

Copper's whistle!
Patrol bell!
Arrest.
Precinct Station.
Iron cell.
Headlines in press:

Man Threatens Landlord
Tenant Held No Bail
Judge Gives Negro 90 Days in County Jail

What Do You Think?

1. Why is this poem entitled "Ballad of the Landlord"? Who is the speaker?
2. How might a landlord respond to this poem?

5. Slum Residents Speak Out*

The following represents testimony before the U.S. Commission on Civil Rights in 1967. All of the speakers in the first section are describing life as they know it— in Cleveland, Ohio; Gary, Indiana; or Boston, Massachusetts.

Excerpted from A Time to Listen. . . A Time to Act. A Report of the National Advisory Commission on Civil Rights, 1967.

"The apartment was very dirty, an undecorated apartment. The plaster in the bathroom was all cracked up . . . and the bathtub, the water dropped by drops, just a drop at a time."

"They move to a building that is a little bit better, a building in which the plumbing is a little less bad, a building in which maybe the roof doesn't leak or a building where you do have some type of toilet facilities. So nobody wants this [deteriorated] building and they left because it is even worse than the one to which they moved. God knows that is bad enough, so it stands there. The landlord won't do anything with it and the city won't do anything with it. It just stands there. . . ."

(Q) "Are rats a problem in your neighborhood?"

(A) "Yes, they are. I was living in one apartment, the rats got in bed with me, and my sister is still living in the same building and the rats are jumping up and down. The kids they play with rats like a child would play with a dog or something. They chase them around the house and things like this."

"I'll tell you when you start complaining about that particular building, no one seems to want to own the building. When I first started to complain. I started with one realty company and I complained so long and loud they sent someone else out and when I complained to him and they sent someone else out . . . Now we complain—it's five of us are complaining now . . . The only time anybody really wants the building is when it is time to pay the rent and after that nobody wants the building."

[The story is little different in Gary, Indiana.]

"Most of the apartments are just rooms. Very few of them have complete baths and hot and cold water, the necessary things, the things that are required healthwise they don't have, very few of them, hot and cold water, heat and this type of thing. You just don't find too many apartments in this area that have this type of thing."

"I mean outside of this district time marches on . . . They build better and they have better but you come down here and you see the same thing year after year after year. People struggling, people wanting, people needing, and nobody to give anyone help."

". . . just like you step in something, you just sink and you can't get out of it. You get in this place and, I don't know, there is something about it that just keeps you. I guess it's the low adequacy of the housing . . . the low morals of the whole place. It's one big nothing. It's one big nothing. I mean you can live here for millions and millions of years and you will see the same place, same time and same situation. It's just like time stops here."

[And in Boston, Massachusetts.]

"[A person] rents a brokendown room for $21 to $24 a week that is rat infested and has cockroaches running all over the place. There are holes in the ceiling where the plaster has fallen down and the people have to share a bathroom. The so-called furnished apartments usually contain a few chairs, a table, and an old rusty bed. . . . Frequently social workers tell families to move out of these homes where the rents are too high, but they never find them decent homes where rents are lower."

"In the section of Roxbury in which I live we have been fighting for street lights for quite some time. But they have completely ignored us. Our street is dark and though we have been writing letters and we have been getting some answers, nothing has happened. I feel it is because this area is predominantly Negro. If it was any other area, they would have gotten action."

"Police have isolated the South End as an area, giving it only token protection. Prostitution, bookmaking and after-hours places are all over and there is an excess of liquor stores and a shortage of foot patrolmen to keep the street safe. A hotel located near police headquarters, and known throughout the city as a house of prostitution, was closed by police after a Boston newspaper publicized it. But it opened again after about two months and is now back in business."

What Do You Think? _____

Some of the testimony hints at a sense of hopelessness that grows up in ghetto slum conditions. Is it possible that this sense of hopelessness could have an influence on continuing such conditions? Explain.

6. How Some Cities Compare*

In 1973 the Urban Institute of Washington, D.C., published results of an on-going research project that has attempted to measure the quality of life in 18 urban areas from coast to coast. See if you can identify the reasons for the rankings.

The study (which in broad terms acknowledges its own deficiencies) completely ignores some traditional measures of the quality of life such as population density, taxes, parks and open space, climate, cultural activities, libraries, other public facilities and the proportion of public service employes to population.

It bases rankings in each category on a lone statistical factor to the exclusion of others which, it might be argued, are equally valid indicators.

Community concern, for example, is based on individual contributions to United Fund charities. Transportation is based on the average cost for a moderate income family of four; it is not concerned with the amount or quality of public transportation, adequacy of highways or average commuting time.

Some of the data on which rankings are based are as much as five years

*San Francisco, Chronicle/Examiner, December 2, 1973.

old; some of the data periods, upon which improvement or deterioration in conditons are measured, range back to 1962. Conclusions, therefore, should be drawn with care.

How 18 Metropolitan Areas Rank in 14 Categories Measuring the Quality of Life, 1962–1973

Metropolitan Area	Unemployment	Poverty	Income Level	Housing	Health	Mental Health	Public Order	Racial Equality	Community Concern	Citizen Participation	Educational Attainment	Transportation	Air Quality	Social Disintegration
Bay Area	16	17	2	14	2	18	13	2	13	7	2	16	1	5
New York	9	9	4	17	9	1	18	1	18	14	9	1	10	7
Los Angeles/ Long Beach	18	15	3	10	2	17	11	3	17	11	3	7	8	3
Chicago	2	5	5	13	18	3	14	6	15	2	7	13	16	1
Philadelphia	7	9	14	9	17	13	6	9	10	8	13	2	15	N.A.
Detroit	17	3	1	5	12	15	17	8	7	5	13	8	14	N.A.
Washington	1	2	8	11	5	7	15	7	16	18	1	10	3	6
Boston	4	1	17	18	6	10	3	N.A.	12	2	6	15	5	4
Pittsburgh	14	12	13	3	11	11	5	5	2	2	13	3	17	N.A.
St. Louis	10	13	12	8	10	4	9	11	6	11	17	14	18	2
Baltimore	5	11	16	4	15	14	4	4	14	14	18	9	11	N.A.
Cleveland	12	7	9	15	8	16	10	12	1	9	9	6	13	N.A.
Houston	5	17	11	1	16	12	12	10	11	16	9	17	5	N.A.
Minneapolis/ St. Paul	14	4	6	6	1	5	7	N.A.	5	1	3	11	2	N.A.
Dallas	3	16	7	2	14	6	8	N.A.	9	16	3	4	3	N.A.
Milwaukee	10	5	15	16	4	8	1	N.A.	8	5	7	4	11	N.A.
Cincinnati	7	14	10	7	7	9	2	N.A.	3	11	13	12	9	N.A.
Buffalo	12	8	18	12	13	2	4	N.A.	4	10	9	18	5	N.A.

N.A.—Not available.

Indicators of Changes in the Quality of Life in the San Francisco Bay Area, 1962–1973

Category	Indicator		Direction of Change in Bay Area
Unemployment	Percent unemployed (1970)		Deteriorating up 8%
	Best: Minn./St. Paul	2.2%	(1969–1970)
	Bay Area:	4.5%	
	Worst: Los Angeles/Long Beach	4.8%	
Educational attainment	Median school years completed (1969)		Improved up .4%
	Best: Washington	12.7	(1967–1969)
	Bay Area:	12.6	
	Worst: Baltimore	11.3	

Category	Indicator		Direction of Change in Bay Area
Poverty	Percent low income households (1970)		Deteriorating up 2%
	Best: Boston	8.6	(1964–1967)
	Worst: Bay Area	16.7	
Health	Infant mortality rate (Per 1000 live births, 1968)		Improved down 3%
	Best: Bay Area	19.3	(1962–1968)
	Worst: Philadelphia	24.8	
Mental health	Reported suicide rate (Per 100,000 pop., 1968)		Same up 1%
	Best: Buffalo	6.1	(1962–1968)
	Worst: Bay Area	23.7	
Racial equality	Unemployment ratio (Nonwhite/white, 1970)		Improved down 13%
	Best: New York	1.2	(1967–1970)
	Bay Area:	1.2	
	Worst: Cleveland	4.0	
Air quality	Concentration of pollutants (1969)		Improved down 3%
	Best: Bay Area		(1964–1969)
	Worst: St. Louis		
Income level	Adjusted per capita income (1969)		Improved up 9%
	Best: Detroit	$4724	(1967–1969)
	Bay Area:	$4635	
	Worst: Buffalo	$3628	
Transportation	Cost to family of four (1969)		Same up .1%
	Best: New York	$ 806	(1967–1969)
	Bay Area:	$ 925	
	Worst: Buffalo	$ 968	
Housing	Cost to family of four (1969)		Deteriorating up 6%
	Best: Houston	$1980	(1967–1969)
	Bay Area:	$2696	
	Worst: Boston	$2976	
Public order	Robberies per 100,000 pop. (1970)		Deteriorating up 33%
	Best: Milwaukee	52	(1964–1970)
	Bay Area:	382	
	Worst: New York	533	
Community concern	United Fund donations (Per capita, 1970)		Improved up 4.6%
	Best: Cleveland	$9.20	(1965–1970)
	Bay Area:	$5.50	
	Worst: New York	$2.20	
Social disintegration	Drug addicts (Per 10,000 pop., 1969)		Not available
	Best: Chicago	31	

41

Table continued

Category	Indicator		Direction of Change in Bay Area
	Bay Area:	59	
	Worst: New York	191	
Citizen participation	Presidential voting rate (1968)		Deteriorating down 5% (1964–1968)
	Best: Minn./St. Paul	76%	
	Bay Area:	67%	
	Worst: Washington	46%	

Here are some examples of what life in the city is like. How do they compare with where you live?

1. The authors of the study clearly state the limits of their research. Why did they do this? Is it important to state the limitations of one's research? Explain.

2. Review the findings of the research. Which facts do you find most interesting? Why?

3. The authors of the study indicate that some of the findings may be out of date. Which ones might these be? Why would anyone publish out-of-date statistics?

4. Which of the pictures seems most typical of city life as you envisage it? Least typical? Why?

---

7. Is Leaving the City the Answer?*

One of the symptoms of the urban crisis in the United States, as well as one of the causes of the flight of people from cities, is the high incidence of city crime. Here is an example of how one couple decided to respond.

For the first 30 years of her life, Ellen Kenwood Gross thought of herself as the essential New Yorker, thriving on the excitement and cultural diversity of the city. She traveled a lot and always looked forward to coming home; she would tell her friends how she wanted to have children and raise them here.

Then, two years ago, the apartment she was living in was burglarized. Six months later she was living in another apartment, and it, too, was looted. Within the next half year the apartment of her fiance, now her husband, was also a target for burglars. And finally, a holdup man broke into her fiance's import business and, after holding a revolver to his throat, ran off with $30.

Mrs. Gross has changed her mind about New York.

In April she and her husband are leaving for the Berkshires, where they have bought an old house.

She has, she says, become intimidated.

"Some of my friends, people who sound just like I used to sound, tell me I ought to stay and fight," she says. "I don't want to stay and fight. I don't feel like fighting at all. If people want to kill each other, let them."

Mrs. Gross recalled how the change came very gradually:

"Before that first burglary, I would hear stories about incidents, but it was always happening to somebody else. It just went in one ear and out the other. I would walk out at any time, even take walks in Central Park at night.

"Some of my friends thought I was crazy," says the Brooklyn-born woman who has lived in a succession of apartments in brownstones on Manhattan's West Side.

*"Manhattan Farewell," *San Francisco Chronicle/Examiner,* February 6, 1973.

"I thought of myself as the typical West Sider, with an interesting job and an active life," she says.

Mrs. Gross stresses these points to underscore her deep commitment to the city and also the radical change in her feelings brought on by fear.

The first sign of this change took place, she says after the first burglary, when the apartment where she had been staying with a woman friend was broken into and a television set and stereo set taken.

"I moved from there and got a perfect West Side apartment in a beautifully renovated brownstone on West End Avenue," she recalls.

"I guess I must have felt something, because after I moved for the first time in my life I had bars put up that I bought for $200 and special locks that cost $100 installed. Friends told me not to bother, if anyone really wanted to get in they could. They were right."

Two months after she moved to a new apartment she was burglarized.

At that time, she and Donald Gross, an importer of Mexican handicrafts, who was her fiance then, would sometimes spin dreams of buying a country house, perhaps just to spend the summer.

Within the six months before their marriage last year Gross' apartment was burglarized twice and he had a gun held to his throat at his offices on New York's Union Square. The dreams took on a new aspect of urgency.

"We knew we would probably be giving up some of the money we are now making and maybe some of our friends, but we would gain much more," she says. "We could leave our door open and we would have time for the important things."

After searching a while they found property in the small town of Otis, Mass., 20 miles from Pittsfield.

What Do You Think? _____

1. Should the Grosses move? Would you if you were in their shoes?
2. Mrs. Gross states that by moving she and her husband "would have time for the important things." What might such "important things" be?

_____

8. Why We Left the City*

From the 1920s on there has been a steady movement in America from the cities to the suburbs. This movement became almost a tidal wave after World War II, when millions of young families with small children took advantage of government-insured mortgages at low rates of interest and bought homes in the areas out-

---

*A California resident.

side our large cities. Why did they go? The following interview will give you some ideas.

Q: When did you move out of the city and into suburbia?
A: It was just after I got out of college—two years after the Korean War ended. I had a job in the city and Shirley wasn't working. The kids were three and five at the time.
Q: Why did you make the move?
A: Well, it was silly to stay in the city. We couldn't afford to buy a house there and paying rent didn't seem to make sense. You never owned anything. Then we saw these places being built only twenty miles from work. There was practically no down payment, the interest rate was low and it was almost like being out in the country—so we bought our first house.
Q: Was it a wise decision?
A: Yes, I'm sure it has been. We were able to sell the first house at a good profit nine years ago and buy this place which we really enjoy. The kids have gone to good schools—they and most of their friends have gone to college so the education has been good. There's less smog down here and, especially with this house, there aren't so many people crowded around. It's a nice friendly neighborhood. We enjoy the occasional parties—so, yes, it's been a wise decision. And one more thing—Shirley has worked for the last five years as an assistant librarian at the local branch of the county library so that's helped financially too.
Q: Any disadvantages?
A: Oh sure. Any time we want to go out we usually go to the city. I like to see a good play periodically; Shirley likes the symphony and the kids have interests in sports and ballet that take them to the city. That usually meant someone had to drive them, though as they got older they used the bus line into town. Yeah, in some ways we're isolated here from a lot that goes on. And it has become increasingly expensive to commute. I can't believe our monthly gasoline bill. I'm thinking seriously of taking the bus. Then the taxes have gone up and up as we've needed more and more services. That may stop since there aren't as many children in the schools now. Couple of other things I don't like, though Shirley doesn't mind too much—the people who live around us are all pretty much the same—same background, same income, same experiences. We don't get much variety. The kids found this out when they went to college. And another thing is I miss the dynamism of the city where so much is happening. There just isn't much going on around here. But on balance I'm glad we've moved to suburbia. We've had a good, even though quiet, life.

What Do You Think?_____

1. What did they give up in leaving the city?
2. Was the decision to move in this case a wise one? Explain your reasoning.

9. What Suburbia Offers

Appeals are still being made for people to move out to suburbia. Would you want to live there?

Before You Spend $40,000 or More for a 4 Bdr. Townhome in Fullerton or Buena Park

See ours. Save $8,000 or More

Los Angeles Times, March 17, 1974.

Suburbia takes many forms—stately mansions and formal gardens, clusters of town-house condominiums, large comfortable homes with a quarter acre of land surrounding them—but the usual suburban form is pictured below. How would you describe it?

1. Compare the pictures of suburbia just presented with those of city life shown on pages 42-43. What differences do you note? Similarities?
2. What might a confirmed city dweller say to a suburbanite? A confirmed suburbanite to a city dweller?

---

10. Suburbanites Have Problems Too*

Suburbia, while it has met some of its early promise, has also run into very real problems. Problems not unlike those which exist in the central cities of the nation . . . and possibly some problems which do not.

Americans who fled big cities by the millions in the past 25 years are finding urban miseries back on their doorsteps—in suburbia.

Their woes are running the full range of those they experienced as city dwellers, from pollution to rising crime, school troubles and high taxes.

Detroit's suburbs, for example, report an increase in residential burglaries, shoplifting and aggravated assault.

Despite a new rapid-transit system in the San Francisco Bay area, commuter tie-ups are worsening. In that city and in others, proposals are being made to limit commuting by automobile as fuel shortages become critical.

In Maryland's Prince Georges County, bordering Washington, D.C., the State has ordered a halt to most sewer construction because of overloaded treatment plants. In nearby Bethesda, Md., air-pollution levels at one intersection exceed those of downtown Washington.

Headlong development in Clayton County outside Atlanta has brought flood erosion and clogged drainpipes. Now county officials may hold building developers responsible for such damage during, and after, construction.

Most of America's suburban communities are getting a sampling of these and other troubles. Hoffman Estates, a white-collar "bedroom community" about 30 miles northwest of Chicago's Loop, is typical of a good many of these communities. For a closer look at how life in suburbia can be—

"Future Shock, Here and Now"

It was only 15 years ago that people began moving to the new development of Hoffman Estates. For most of them it meant escape from Chicago's dirt, troubled schools, unsafe streets and escalating taxes.

*"Problems Invade Suburbs," reprinted from *U.S. News & World Report,* December 10, 1973. Copyright © 1973, U.S. News & World Report, Inc.

Today, Hoffman Estates is a community of 32,500 people—and their dream of spacious living is beginning to wear thin at the edges.

As vacant land becomes scarcer and more valuable, apartment buildings and town-house complexes are springing up in the midst of single-family homes—overloading existing facilities such as schools. Additional dwelling projects are on the way.

Future deterioration is casting its shadow—even during a development boom—as paint fades and peels on some of the older homes in Hoffman Estates.

During commuting hours, automobiles are lined up bumper to bumper on feeder streets leading into the Northwest Tollway that bisects the town. Village streets are torn up in the endless race against mounting congestion of traffic.

Says Mayor Virginia Hayter:

"We're getting future shock, here and now."

As an era of agonizing reappraisal dawns for Hoffman Estates—and hundreds of other American suburbs—most of its people say they are still reasonably satisfied with the quality of life they are getting now. But they worry that "future shock," for them, is just beginning. Estimates are that Hoffman Estates will double its population by 1980.

Textbook of troubles: A summing up of their concern comes from Mrs. Felice Miller, wife of an air-traffic controller.

Four years ago, when she and her family moved to the suburbs, "you could look for miles and see nothing but farmland." With population becoming denser, she said, "There's no benefit to living here any more." She adds:

"We've heard people describe the apartment complexes as a tumor engulfing the whole area. The people are O.K., but these apartments crowd the schools and raise taxes."

As planners see it, Hoffman Estates is becoming a textbook example of the troubles that are afflicting U.S. suburbs laid out years ago with little thought for the future or for people's needs.

Fifteen years after its launching, Hoffman Estates still appears on the map as an incomplete jigsaw puzzle, composed of several developments—single homes, town houses or apartments—separated by diminishing parcels of land.

The community was designed by the original developer as a few tracts of housing. Other developments came along, haphazardly, over the years.

Result: Hoffman Estates has remained a "bedroom town" with settlements separated from each other. It has a few small shopping plazas but no central business area. Even its new city hall occupies, in splendid isolation, the middle of an otherwise empty field. Remarks one resident:

"We're victims of the shopping-center madness out here. We came along too late to have a traditional downtown—I don't think one was ever envisioned."

The lack of community core bears visible results. To visitors, Hoffman Estates is the archetype of the anonymous suburb, its scaled-down ranch houses and colonials merging without notice into neighboring Schaumburg. **49**

One home-owner admits cheerfully: "You could drive straight through Hoffman Estates—and never know you'd been here."

Many—but not all—residents say they don't mind the lack of distinction. More than a few share the attitude of Joseph Zeller, 33, an advertising executive who says:

"I don't spend enough time in Hoffman Estates even to know what's going on. To me this is a bedroom community. I'm just here to sack out."

That mood of indifference was jolted recently when two ex-mayors of Hoffman Estates and two former village trustees—equivalent to city councilmen—pleaded guilty to charges of bribery, conspiracy and tax evasion in connection with a major rezoning that opened the way to a town-house complex.

More Density In Traffic and Housing

It is not corruption, but other worries that are pressing in most urgently on the people of Hoffman Estates.

Crowded schools, roads: At a time when many U.S. communities find their school costs tapering off as the birth rate declines, Hoffman Estates is putting out more money on schools because of growing population.

The Schaumburg elementary-school district, serving both communities, opened two new schools this autumn, is building two more and is awaiting bids on two others.

Already education accounts for 60 percent of the tax bite on Hoffman Estate home-owners—and may soon account for more. The school district is adding 800 new students a year, and may double the present enrollment of 15,000 before the end of the 1970's.

Because Hoffman Estates, unlike neighboring Schaumburg, lacks extensive business properties, its school costs fall disproportionately on home-owners, who are paying property taxes higher than those within Chicago and all but 10 of Cook County's 17 suburbs.

More irritating to some people, on a day-by-day basis, is traffic congestion far beyond anything envisioned by most residents a few years ago. The village's major link to the rest of metropolitan Chicago—the six-lane Northwest Tollway—becomes progressively more crowded.

Today, a breadwinner heading for home from the Loop on Friday afternoons can spend an hour negotiating the first 10 miles of the 30-mile journey in combat on the expressway not only with thousands of other suburbanites but with airline passengers bound for giant O'Hare Airport—located halfway between downtown Chicago and Hoffman Estates. King-size traffic jams are developing on village roads, too.

Police Chief John O'Connell reports that cars now are lined up for half a mile, morning and evening, at one intersection. A woman commenting on how "eerie and quiet" Hoffman Estates could be just a few years ago, says she declines invitations to visit friends several miles away in late afternoon because "it's no use trying to fight that traffic."

Land prices: Because Hoffman Estates is in the middle ring of suburbs surrounding Chicago, with some land still available, land values have shot up —to the point where single-family homes no longer are feasible in the $25,000 category. Says one real-estate agent:

"Five years ago, new, single-family homes were being sold for $20,000. Today that same house in Hoffman Estates would cost $35,000, newly built. Builders are spending $20,000 an acre for land they once could buy for $1,000. You can't build a $20,000 house on such property any more."

Nor do builders show any interest in putting up $50,000 homes in a community whose socioeconomic profile was set irreversibly 15 years ago at a much different level. What they are doing, instead, is salvaging the $25,000 market among young, middle-class families by putting up condominium apartments or closely packed town houses—which, in turn, are multiplying Hoffman Estates' automobiles, sewage costs, outlays on fire and police protection, spending on schools and tax levies.

Although few of the older residents talk of leaving, their resentment of the newcomers and disquiet over the future are becoming evident.

One woman says she and her husband are increasingly uneasy about the development boom, convinced it is turning their village into "another close-in suburb, which is what we came here to get away from." She goes on:

"Not many people sit down and ask what this township will be like a few years from now. One reason is that many of us don't expect to be here to confront that fact."

Ignored, excluded: Apartment and town-house dwellers themselves are becoming resentful over the feeling of being slighted by civic and government officials, and excluded from some of the community activities and organizations. A former apartment renter, Mrs. Karen Murphy of Baton Rouge, La., says:

"It's growing so fast, people come and go so fast, you don't get involved in lasting relationships. Nobody wants to help you, even in the stores. Did we expect too much?"

Hoffman Estates' youngsters also are said to be feeling estrangement from the community. Bryan Styer, the village's 23-year-old director of youth services, reports lethargy among the teen-agers because they have fewer things to do than is the case with Chicago youngsters.

Furthermore, he notes, youths in Hoffman Estates and nearby suburbs are being exposed to more illegal drugs, at an earlier age, than was the case three years ago. Mr. Styer says he now sees instances of drug usage among seventh and eighth graders. He adds:

"It's easier to stay alienated here than in the city because of the transportation problem. In a city, you have everyone more or less at your doorstep, and live very close to many other people."

The Fight Against Rampant Growth

Across the nation, suburbs such as Hoffman Estates are pondering answers to the question: Is a downhill slide into stagnation and blight inevitable for troubled communities that ring America's big cities?

In the San Francisco Bay area, suburbs are frantically taking measures to acquire open space—and keep it open despite pressures from developers. The town of Petaluma, 40 miles north of San Francisco, has imposed a limit of 500 new homes a year. To the east, the towns of Pleasanton and Fremont brought a runaway building boom to a halt by forming a group known as "Save All Valley Environment" (SAVE) which got voter approval to curtail construction.

The State of Florida now requires developers of large projects—including residential, business and industrial tracts—to file detailed statements on the impact of such projects on environment, natural resources, economy, public facilities, transportation and housing of surrounding regions.

Elsewhere, suburbs are stiffening zoning laws or holding up construction of utilities that new subdivisions need. Some even require builders to provide parks and libraries.

However, many suburbs are finding money scarce for buying up open space and taking other measures to curb runaway growth. And an official of the National Association of Counties points to another problem: "People who came to the suburbs wanted to forget about urban troubles."

Citizen indifference is only one of several obstacles that Hoffman Estates officials are having to overcome in their fight to stave off deterioration and, eventually, decay.

New regime: Mayor Hayter and some other reformists were elected to the village board of trustees in a voter rebellion four years ago against the board's action in rezoning land to permit the building of 10,000 apartment units—an action which brought on the recent indictments against former trustees.

Since then, she has kept the municipal tax rate from increasing, involved scores of citizens in municipal activities and renegotiated with developers to hold down building density. New developers are screened carefully for reputation and management policies before getting permission to build.

Roadblocks are plentiful, however, in the fight to keep out uncontrolled growth.

Forty per cent of the land within Hoffman Estates is county-controlled forest preserve, beyond the control of the village board. Zoning rights for high-density housing, once granted, cannot normally be revoked when rising costs of construction make single-family homes economically impossible to build for the medium-price market.

Furthermore, the property owners and officials of Hoffman Estates can do little about conflict in land-use policy with the neighboring village of Schaumburg, which is allowing four 12-floor apartment buildings to rise across the street from a subdivision of single-family homes in Hoffman Estates.

Perhaps the toughest problem Mayor Hayter confronts is that of getting newcomers in high-density housing areas interested in checking headlong growth. Says one resident:

"Those of us living in the town houses, and apartment complexes are in a separate little world. We've got our own golf courses, clubs, swimming pools and even snow removal, garbage pickup and street repairs—all independent of the rest of the town. I think the isolation accounts for the low voter turnout from these places for village election."

Mayor Hayter herself virtually concedes defeat in arousing civic spirit in the new developments.

"If people regard Hoffman Estates as a way station toward someplace else, we can't force them to be active in the community," she said.

Nonetheless, she intends to keep trying.

The extent to which Mayor Hayter and her colleagues succeed may measure the prospects that America's suburbs will eventually regain at least a small slice of the Utopia to which many suburbanites were looking ahead fondly when they packed up and moved out of the nation's big cities during the years after World War II.

What Do You Think? _____

1. What city problems have become suburban problems?

2. What do suburbanites mean when they say that they think "future shock" for them is just beginning? How might such "future shock" be avoided?

3. Many people argue that the future movement of people will be "up rather than out." What do you think they mean?

4. Do people who move to suburbia "expect too much"? Explain. How can civic spirit be developed in suburban areas like Hoffman Estates—or can it?

---

11. Renewed Interest in the City: Two Views

In 1974 there were indications of renewed interest in the city as a place of business and as a residence. Yet, in 1975, New York City verged on bankruptcy. Here are opinions on how New York, and other cities with comparable problems, might be helped.

Can the City Make it?*

Don't count out America's cities.

That is the message from New York, which appears at least to be stemming the past few years' near-disastrous flight of businesses from the city to the suburbs . . . and beyond.

Already:

- The somber list of companies packing their corporate crates for New Jersey, Connecticut, St. Louis, Dallas, and elsewhere is growing shorter. It is a reassuringly compact list compared with the late '60's and early '70's.
- The ranks of companies remaining, expanding, or moving in, are swelling.

Credit Rating Raised

- The outflow of jobs in the past five years has been slowed to a comparative trickle.
- And Standard & Poors has just raised the city's credit rating to an "A" —the green-light signal to investors across the nation. This favorable rating signifies confidence in the city's handling of its finances, enables the city to attract bond buyers at lower interest rates, and gives the city's overall economic climate a welcome boost.

No one here is certain that this delicate improvement, carefully nurtured by the recently departed Lindsay administration, will last. A prolonged transit strike, a new crime wave, revived racial unrest, could set it back.

But Mayor Abraham D. Beame seems determined to keep momentum up.

Landmark Decision: "The importance of maintaining and expanding business here and of attracting new business cannot be overemphasized," the new Mayor said firmly at a Jan. 16 gathering during which the Radio Corporation of America (RCA) announced its landmark decision to stay in its traditional Rockefeller Center home rather than move to neighboring Connecticut.

Giving his words more force, the Mayor announced Jan. 21 the formation of a coalition of powerful business, labor, and civic leaders whose aim will be to keep business in the city as well as reaching out for newcomers.

Companies are recognizing that "they can't run away from the problems" of the city, says Thomas N. Stainback, president of the New York Chamber of Commerce, since the problems "are now spilling into the suburbs."

Revolutionary Facility: Among those committed to remain or expand in the city, besides RCA, which is constructing a revolutionary conference facility powered in part by solar energy atop a wing of Rockefeller Center, are Sears Roebuck & Co., Harper & Row Publishers, Inc., Sony Corporation, J. C. Penney Company, Inc.

Norton Simon, Inc., Schlumberger, Ltd., U.S. Homes, Marsh & McLennan, Inc., are some of those moving into the city.

The changed climate is reflected, too, in jobs. "I feel rather silly saying we've only lost 20,000 jobs last year," admits Herbert Bienstock, assistant director of the Bureau of Labor Statistics.

But, he explains, the figure was 49,000 for the previous year and 135,000 for the year before that. So 20,000 represents "relative stabilization."

Return to the Cities—A Trend that's Picking up Speed*

Are suburbia's troubles causing a retreat of whites back to the big cities?

Not yet on a major scale, municipal planners conceded—but some insist that the groundwork for such a development is being established in the small but definite trickle of middle-class whites into cities after years of suburban exile.

Big-city officials are predicting that this trickle will enlarge as the fuel shortage makes commuting more difficult—encouraging people who have been planning an eventual move back to the cities to take the plunge now rather than waiting.

Some are older couples whose children have married and moved away. But growing numbers are young couples—often with both husband and wife working—who can afford urban housing and entertainment such as theaters, restaurants or concerts. Said a real-estate broker in Washington, D.C., where Georgetown and Capitol Hill have become prime examples of urban renovation:

"A lot of these young people grew up in the suburbs and are rebelling against the kind of uniformity they grew up with. Cities have always been magnets to the young, and the fact that so many of them now put off having children, and then have only one or two, makes it economically feasible for them to live well in the city."

Moving Back. Philadelphia and Boston may be the only two cities actually getting a net inflow of middle-class Americans. But the trickle into the cities from the suburbs appears to be gaining in some other places too.

In New Orleans' inner city, an area once inhabited by the very rich and the very poor, middle-income white families are moving in to take advantage of the growing availability of moderately priced housing—mainly apartments.

Young marrieds, especially, are buying and restoring old houses in the French Quarter and neighboring areas. One lure: New Orleans' excellent bus system which has a 15-cent basic fare—one of the lowest in the nation.

Atlanta's Inman Park, which was the city's first residential suburb, in the mid-nineteenth century, is becoming a focal point for migrants from the suburbs as well as for young couples buying their first home. Inman Park had deteriorated into a slum neighborhood where "winos" slept in the front yards of rundown mansions.

In Memphis, about 250 houses have been restored in the Central Garden section, 10 minutes from downtown.

Newcomers to the inner area of Savannah have reclaimed 800 residential buildings in eight years. Reid Williamson, Jr., executive vice president of the Historic Savannah Foundation, Inc., is a former Atlanta suburbanite who rejoices over this release from two hours of grass-cutting every week-end.

*Reprinted from *U.S. News & World Report,* December 10, 1973. Copyright © 1973, U.S. News & World Report, Inc.

"Getting to work from the suburbs took an hour," he recalls. "Here, I'm a seven-minute walk from downtown."

Similarly, Boston's South End, whose 3,000 row houses degenerated into a rooming-house area nearly a century ago and later became a center of crime and prostitution, is being repopulated by middle-class couples. Renovation, much of it done by individuals with the help of low-interest loans from the city's redevelopment authority, is resulting in attractive or even elegant homes, costing as much as $85,000 on today's market.

And New Homes. Some renovation is going on in New York City's upper west side, but planners pin their hopes on construction of middle-income and luxury apartments and homes—20,000 units last year. Developers report growing applications for housing from suburban counties, and the City Planning Commission reports that the exodus of whites from the city is diminishing sharply.

Planners note that "middle class" is a term applying to growing numbers of blacks who are establishing attractive enclaves[1] in such cities as Los Angeles and Atlanta. In some of Detroit's integrated neighborhoods, they are working with white home-owners to discourage racial turnover. In Wilmington, Del., Negroes are in the forefront of "urban homesteaders," who buy city-owned houses for $1 and gain title after living in them for a year and renovating them.

In Portland, Ore., Mayor Neil Goldschmidt is promoting a drive to keep people in the city by neighborhood improvement. Eventually he hopes to lure people from outlying areas with a housing project on the Willamette River.

Over the long haul, urban specialists see conditions favoring a return to health for cities. In the near future, they point out, pollution controls and curbs on use of cars may lengthen commuting time by forcing suburbanites to take mass-transit vehicles.

Furthermore, they add the low birth rate of today means more couples who can afford city living—even if it requires paying for private schooling for their youngsters. Such young marrieds, the experts say, will be more and more likely to choose city living as suburban problems start outweighing the advantages many people thought they were getting when they fled from the cities.

What Do You Think? _____

1. What factors in particular might be causing a renewed interest among people and corporations to live and work in the city?

2. Since 1974 the financial status of New York City declined so precipitously that the city was on the verge of default. Only federal and state aid saved the situation, after the city instituted emergency measures. What measures would you suggest to restore a city's economic health?

3. Which of the following groups in each category would be most inclined to live in a city rather than a suburb? Explain your reasoning.

[1]A minority group culture living as an entity.

Age	Income	Race	Sex
18–20 year olds	under $7,000	whites	males
21–30	$7,000–$15,000	nonwhites	females
31–50	$25,000–$50,000		
51 and over	over $50,000		

12. What Kind of City Do We Want?*

The quality of life in the city has been a matter of controversy for centuries. August Hecksher notes some similarities between ancient Greek discussions and our problems today. What kind of city do you want?

In the building of a city, as in the making of a life, attitudes are more important than economics; and cities and human lives, like all works of art, are fundamentally made by belief. I have been reminded of this as I have traveled a bit about the country, seeing what is happening to the places where men live and work.

There are cities that under the pressures of an immense common determination are remaking themselves; and there are cities that quite literally are being thrown away. In the latter case people who can afford to move out, do so; those who manage to lift themselves above the deeper levels of want slip into the dwelling places of those who have gone. Then they themselves stage an evacuation. They leave behind, like a disposable plastic jar, the city that had been the center of men's hopes.

The contrast is, as I have suggested, a contrast of cities; but in a deeper sense it is a contrast of human beliefs. In every city, to put the matter more fairly and accurately, there are men and women who are committed to the civitas,[1] and there are those who seek in escape an easier, cleaner, simpler existence. I might even say that in every individual there are these same opposing tendencies. At moments we rejoice in the excitement and conflict of the forum; at other moments we imagine for ourselves the pleasures of a romantically pastoral life. By turns we are a man of the urb and of the sub-urb.

Now these contradictory tendencies are very old, and indeed were the subject of lively controversy among the Greek philosophers. Having drawn so many of our ideas about reason and truth from them, we might just as well seek some light on the contemporary city. In "The Republic" Plato presents what appears to be the image of an ideal community, built to satisfy the natural needs of man. Farmers and craftsmen are its chief citizens, along with a

*The Two Cities," by August Hecksher, *The Christian Science Monitor,* March 22, 1974.
[1]City life.

sprinkling of traders and shopkeepers. In their leisure hours they are content to recline on branches of yew and myrtle strewn upon the ground, and to feast on olives and cheese, with figs and roasted acorns for dessert. Things seem to be going swimmingly in this first city, and Socrates declares it to be "the true and healthy one."

But Plato has someing else in mind. He causes Glaucon to denounce this simple community as "a city of pigs," and to praise the modern style where the citizens lie on courches, dine off tables, and eat many sweets. This is the second, or "luxurious" city. It has its drawbacks, but it is the more rational home of man, and Plato devotes the next eight books of "The Republic" to that great search for justice which shall make such a city truly habitable.

In the next century the philosopher Epicurus once more takes up the cudgels for the simple life of the First City. By then he sees Athens as corrupt. He spurns the life of political commitment, and sets up himself and his school outside the town, in a House and a Garden. I had always supposed the garden to be a bower, an idyllic retreat, at least a sort of park; but Dr. Benjamin Farrington in his "The Faith of Epicurus" tells us it was really a kitchen garden, a place for growing cabbages, radishes, turnips, leeks and cucumbers. However that may be, the House and its Garden represented a challenge to Plato's "luxurious city"; and there, in place of Justice, Epicurus set up the ideal of Friendship. Friendship, said he, in a sentence that may delight some of our younger radicals, "goes dancing round the world bidding us all awake and pass on the salutation of blessedness."

One cannot, I suppose, carry these old controversies too far, not apply them too literally to the modern condition. ("City of pigs"—that is a strong epithet, and one which I hope none of my readers will assume I am applying to his estate!) Those who stand fast today to maintain and rebuild our central cities, imagining high-rise developments, with aerial bridges, rapid transit systems, splendid plazas, are no doubt driven as much by self-interest as by a vision. And those who flee, far from dreaming of a philosopher's garden, are too often in search of the meagerest decencies of existence.

Nevertheless, and in the end, we are going to have to make our choice between the two cities—at least between the illusion of the simple city and the hopes of the complex or "luxurious" city. I must admit to being on the side of the latter. I cannot believe that late in this twentieth century, with its wealth of science and all its Protean[2] possibilities, we are simply going to walk away from the city centers and try to forget them. In Europe after World War II, when it seemed the fierce bombings had left a soil from which nothing would grow, the great cities rose again miraculously from the rubble. There is a life in every city that has embodied the dreams and ambitions of man, waiting only to be touched by those who believe.

Friendship is fine, we might say in answer to Epicurus; but it is in the search for Justice—for harmony amid the contradictions of rich and varied existence—that man has reached his height.

58   [2]Various.

What Do You Think?

Mr. Hecksher is very optimistic about the city. Do you share his optimism. Why or why not?

ACTIVITIES FOR INVOLVEMENT

1. Check the latest census of your area (either the 1970 census or a special one since that time) and attempt to develop data on your city's housing. Check the number of dilapidated houses and those without all facilities. Make a chart that indicates the figures on such conditions.

2. From the data you have developed and from your reading, formulate your recommendations for a sound housing policy by (a) the federal government, (b) the state government, and (c) the local government.

3. Organize a work team and visit the office of your city planner. Develop a time study of how he spends his day. What kinds of special problems must he deal with aside from just planning your city's future growth?

4. Contact the local real estate association and invite a representative to come to your classroom. Get his or her views on housing and what should be done about the housing problem of our central cities.

5. Some people argue that there is no racial discrimination involved in the urban housing problem. Others claim that much of the problem is caused by the refusal of whites to sell to blacks or to lend them money with which to make home purchases. With which opinion do you agree? Conduct an investigation in your area to see if you can find evidence of discrimination.

6. People often base decisions upon beliefs rather than upon knowledge. Prepare a list of your beliefs about the suburbs and another list of actual facts. From your lists, attack or defend the idea "The suburban way of life is best."

4
TRANSPORTATION: CAN YOU GET THERE FROM HERE?

Have you ever been on the freeway at 5:30 in the evening as people attempted to hurry home from work and shopping? Have you ever tried to find a parking place downtown in order to run in and make a small purchase? Have you ever attempted to drive from downtown to the airport and find a parking place close to the terminal?

It is an oddity of our time that the simple actions above often take longer time than a flight of 500 miles. We are able to move quickly over relatively long distances, whereas local traffic is increasingly snarled. Both situations pose a problem for our cities.

Americans love their automobiles. Somehow the family auto has become symbolic of freedom, of the ability to get somewhere, anywhere the driver wishes to go. For this reason, and because we have not as yet had time to build really modern rapid transit systems that can compete in either cost or total convenience with the auto, the freeways leading to our largest cities are clogged to overflowing morning and evening. While highway construction projects multiply, the auto industry continually increases production to keep up with the rising demand for new cars.

We seem to be caught in a vicious cycle. The more cars there are on the road, the greater is the demand for highways and parking. As highways have grown to freeways and as entire blocks of the central city have turned into parking lots, the increased ease of driving has encouraged more and more people to use their cars. The response in some areas—Cleveland and the San Francisco Bay area, for example—has been to build rapid transit systems that hopefully will decrease auto traffic.

In some cities there has been a revolt by the citizens against the destruction of homes and living space by the freeway builders. City residents fear that their cities will become mainly highways and parking lots—even to the point where there will no longer be any reason to come to the city.

For long trips Americans are turning more and more to the air. Passenger trains are rapidly becoming a thing of the past. The great increase in air travel has created several problems for cities. Location of air terminals, control of air traffic, and access to air terminals are only three of the difficulties now being faced by city planners and transportation experts.

A future problem which will cause many headaches (literally) will be the noise of the supersonic planes as they go through the sound barrier.

Although there are many different systems of transportation, it is important that we look at transportation as one problem. The difficulties of the commuter become the difficulties of the international traveler as he attempts to go from the airport to the city. The problems of building a rapid transit system which will compete in efficiency and comfort with the private auto become the problems of millions of citizens who must pay taxes and support the system.

We shall examine some of these dilemmas next.

---

1. Things Aren't What They Used to Be*

Less than 60 years ago a trip by auto across country was a real adventure. Today it is rather commonplace. Remember that in no other 60-year period in all of history have such changes occurred in our means of transporting ourselves. Would a trip like the one described below be possible today?

In 1915, when I was a boy, I was invited to go along when a benevolent uncle undertook a drive from Minneapolis to Los Angeles. . . . [My] uncle took along a truck full of tents, cots, and so on. We camped along the way, all the way, partly because it was fun but mostly because in all the world there was not a motel, a tourist cabin, or a trailer park. The empty yards that surrounded country schoolhouses made good camping sites, as I recall it: there was plenty of room, and there were sanitary facilities of a sort. In the emptier reaches of Wyoming and Nevada the party simply pulled off the road and camped in the sagebrush.

Finding the way was sometimes a problem, because there were no road maps and no route numbers. Our party had three cars—two touring cars and that truck—and the lead car carried packets of confetti; when it made a turn at a fork in the road, it tossed out a few handfuls so that the following cars would know which turn to take. The cars usually stayed half a mile apart, because between Minneapolis and San Francisco, there was not one mile of paved road outside of the cities and the dust a car could leave behind it was something to experience. All of the women in the parties wore long linen dusters, and the men wore khaki. Most of us wore goggles as a matter of routine.

I mentioned "touring cars." They were open cars with collapsible tops, carrying side curtains which could be buttoned in place if it rained. The closed car with glass windows was strictly for city driving then; those bumpy roads would have shattered the glass in short order on a cross-country trip. It may be in place to mention that my uncle had a chauffeur, who was very busy every

*Excerpted from the introduction to "Ocean to Ocean—by Automobile," by Bruce Catton, *American Heritage,* April 1962. Copyright © 1962 by American Heritage Publishing Co., Inc. Reprinted by permission.

single evening adjusting the motors, repairing tires, and doing other things that made it possible for us to keep moving. Flat tires, of course, were literally everyday affairs.

Nobody hurried on a cross-country trip. We averaged about one hundred miles a day, which was considered a bit leisurely but not very much so. It might be remembered that most of the roads between Iowa and California were all but totally unimproved. You couldn't make time on such roads if you wanted to, and if you tried you quickly broke something—a spring, a hip, or something.

Obviously this was not much like motoring today. It was a great deal less comfortable, but somehow it was more fun. And some of us who are now doddering peacefully down the sunset slope look back on those days with a queer fondness. You can do absolutely anything with a car nowadays—except do what we did back before the First World War.

What Do You Think?

1. The trip described was not like motoring today, "but somehow it was more fun." What do you think the author had in mind when he made this statement? Would you agree with him? Explain.

2. Could you make a similar kind of journey today?

2. Advantages and Disadvantages of the Automobile*

It is clear from the following article that the automobile has a great many advantages for its user. Might this dependence on the automobile be lessened in any way?

What is there in the automobile's hold on the public that could be usefully incorporated in transit planning?

- An origin-to-destination method of transportation.
- Normally available at all times.
- Goes in any direction at the whim of the driver.
- Doesn't have to stop and pick up others.
- Provides privacy and reasonable safeguards against the annoyance of others.

No other method of transportation since the horse and buggy has afforded such advantages to the individual driver and his family.

*Jarald A. Kieffer, "The Automobile's Success: A Lesson for Its Critics," *The Futurist,* February 1973.

What about the disadvantages?

- The internal combustion engine is very inefficient, fouls the air, wastes costly fuel.
- Cars waste space, frequently run with only one occupant, are often larger than their function requires.
- Cars must be stored at the end of a trip, the cost of garages and carports must be added to that of houses and buildings.
- Expensive urban land is used for parking, streets are congested by parked cars.
- Expensive to buy, operate and repair, value depreciates at a rate which makes the car relatively one of the worst investments people can make.
- Drivers attempt to handle cars with widely varying capacities and skills, often with permanently or temporarily defective powers of judgment.
- In motion under certain weather conditions, the car can become a nearly uncontrollable terror.

In the eyes of the auto user, the advantages appear to outweigh the disadvantages. The auto user's attachment to his machine has a fairly substantial emotional base. It would have to be emotional because it is plain that the average driver is aware of the mounting evidence that the continued use of cars under present city conditions is becoming almost counter-productive to him and to his community.

So far, extensive regulatory effort against cars has not been successful. Instead we see the sheer mass of automobiles increasing and spreading. Transit alternatives now exist and deserve full and urgent public examination and governmental encouragement. We have it within our current technical capacities to shape the kind of transit development we want and need, development that would be responsive to people's needs. The key lies not just in the type of vehicles to be used but in the whole concept of convenience and accessibility to the public.

A very promising solution to our urban transportation problems may well lie in developing a concept of mass transit that offers the peculiar advantages of the automobile and avoids many of the disadvantages.

We can provide mass transit on a near origin-to-destination basis. It is not a simple problem, but we already have the technology and know-how to solve it.

The whole future of our urban concentrations, including their very feasibility and the quality and meaning of life within them, may well depend directly on our ability to head off expected increases in auto usage in the years ahead. This need, plus the simple humanity of providing transportation to those who do not now have adequate access to it, give all the justification that is required.

Transit planners must step back and take another look at how the mass of Americans want to move in and around their urban areas. Planning that fails to do this is wasteful and useless. Planning that tends to emphasize the

needs of the technical system of transit rather than the needs of the people will lead to public rejection of the plans, or to rejection of the transit system if built over their objections. We have the technical know-how to provide adequate people-oriented urban transportation. In terms of attracting the public to transit, we would do well to take as a starting point the most attractive personal features that drew the American to the automobile.

What Do You Think?

1. Do the advantages of the automobile outweigh its disadvantages? Why or why not?
2. What might a non-auto user say to the owner of an automobile?
3. Do most automobile owners have an "emotional attachment" to their autos? Is this good or bad? Can it be lessened in any way? Should it be?

3. What About the Subway?*

Mexico City's experience with a rather "old-fashioned" form of transportation has been encouraging. The Mexico City Metro has become a show place, the center for community life, and a very rapid means of transportation.

All over the world the much-abused underground railway has been making a comeback as the only solution to urban congestion and commuter chaos —and now also to the energy crisis. And the most striking new example of the success of an underground (or metro or subway) is not in any of the rich cities of Europe or the United States, but in the teeming metropolis of Mexico.

The shining new metro of Mexico City is not only efficient and beautiful; it actually makes a profit. Last month a contract was signed to extend its lines further out to the suburbs of this city of 8 million people. With its boldness and flare, it has much to teach the shabby old systems of New York, London or Paris.

The idea of the underground was first developed in mid-19th Century London, to avoid the horse-drawn traffic jams of the Victorian City. It was then a heroic innovation, full of daring engineering and elegant cast-iron decorations.

Later in the century, the Paris Metro extended the creative scope, with those curling art-nouveau entrance arches which are now collectors' pieces in expensive antique shops.

But the old metropolitan railways became shabby, dirty and despised— and the newest extension in London, the Victoria Line, shows little innovation and hardly any aesthetic sense.

The New York subway is a standing disgrace to the richest city in the

*San Francisco Chronicle/Examiner, February 10, 1974, "This World" section.

world. Its fierce, rattling trains and filthy platforms are enlivened by the bright graffiti sprayed on the carriages by enterprising delinquents.

The French have shown more recent inspiration, as for instance in their elegant new Louvre station in Paris. But it is abroad, away from the restrictions of their own capital, that the French engineers have found a fuller challenge, most notably in building the new metros in Montreal and—more spectacularly—in Mexico City.

The secret of the Mexico City metro is that it treats underground transportation not as a regrettable necessity, like sewers or lavatories, but as an exciting extension of the living city and its monuments. It does more than move people; it adds a new dimension to the city above it.

Its success rests on a marriage of French engineers and Mexican designers. The contract for building it was won by the French as part of their drive for trade with Latin America, and the basic concept is unmistakably based on the original Paris Metro, leading to wide platforms just under street level, with automatic doors on the platforms which shut when the trains arrive.

But the old pattern has been brought up to date, with comfortable carriages which glide on rubber wheels, and the Mexican genius for gay design has been exploited to the fullest. The underground spaces and concourses have been used as an opportunity not for pomp and chandeliers, like the Moscow metro, but for bazaars, exhibitions and even archaeology.

A connection between one metro line and another is not (as in Paris or London) a bleak, windy passage but an underground bazaar with bright stalls on either side, and amongst them an ancient pillar, uncovered in the excavations, is lit up as a showpiece.

Underneath the historic center of Mexico City, the "zocalo" (square) in front of the cathedral, where both Montezuma and Cortez once held court, there is now a wide underground square, filled with models of the buildings above, and with plans of the city.

One station, the Bellas Artes, which serves the city's exuberant[1] opera house, is a special tour de force,[2] a complete underground sculptural gallery, taking the principle of the Louvre station in Paris to its logical extension.

The platforms and walls of the station are of polished marble, and along the walls are plausible[3] reproductions of Mayan or Aztec carvings and statues, copied from the Mexican national collection. The exhibition continues into the passages and entrances, so that a traveler can acquire an artistic education while he waits.

The statues have not been defaced with initials, slogans or obscenities: the dignity of the platforms, like an actual art gallery, provides its own awe.

Above ground, the building of the metro has been the opportunity for refashioning some of the messier parts of the city.

One station, The Isurgents, has now become part of a cheerful new pedestrian precinct built in the middle of a busy roundabout of traffic.

There is a circle of open-air cafes, loud with trumpets and violins, with passages leading up to the intersecting streets and down to the metro.

At each station, the bright sign of the "M" shines out, with below it the special symbol of the station, and the symbols continue underground and in the carriages to guide illiterates and tourists to their destinations.

When Mexicans receive foreign politicians and dignitaries to their city, they like to insist that they visit not only the pyramids, the cathedral and anthropological museum, but also take a ride on the metro.

What Do You Think? _____

1. How feasible are subways for use in all cities?
2. What advantages are there to subways? Disadvantages? What is the chief advantage of the Mexico City subway?

---

4. Or High-Speed Trains?*

Modern technology, too, is assisting in solving some of our transportation problems. The French have been among the pioneers in developing land travel technology, and now they are working on a radically new, but simple, air cushion train. Here is a report on their progress.

Have you ever wanted to rise on a cushion of air, without the shake, rattle and roll of the traditional railroad track? The French are well on their way

[1]Lively.
[2]Stroke of genius.
[3]Believable.
*Michael Sullivan, "This World" section, *San Francisco Examiner/Chronicle,* February 10, 1974. **67**

to providing Parisians with cushion-smooth travel and, if they're successful, one day you may find your commuter special more luxurious than a public relations man's dream.

Backers of the air cushion concept say it's a far better mode of transport than the old-fashioned wheeled vehicle. With none of the friction resistance of the wheel, it can go virtually as fast as a plane.

For the same reason, it requires less power to move forward.

The principle of the air cushion, developed by French engineer Jean Bertin, is disarmingly simple. Some say it is the first technological breakthrough in vehicle support since the wheel. This is the way it works:

Blowers pump air down through ducts in the bottom of the chassis, raising the vehicle off the ground. The car sits astride a monorail shaped like an upside down "T" that serves as a railroad track. For propulsion, engineers mount a linear motor on the vehicle that takes its forward motion from contact with the central guide rail much like a subway's third rail.

There is almost no limit to the speed or distance that the Aerotrain, developed by Societé de l'Aerotrain, can travel. The cash-short French government chose the run between La Defense, just outside Paris, with the fast-growing suburb of Cergy-Pontoise, 14 miles to the northwest, because it is so heavily traveled. It is also badly in need of rail service.

All that's needed now is a decision by the French government to go ahead with construction. If the government says "go," the $60 million track will whisk up to 10,000 persons an hour between Cergy and La Defense at speeds of up to 100 miles an hour.

France is not the only site for an eventual Aerotrain track. Societe de l'Aerotrain has formed a joint venture with a company based in Chula Vista, California. The group, with $12 million from the U.S. Department of Transportation, is presently working on development of an air-cushion vehicle tailored to U.S. needs. Tests are being carried out on a track at Pueblo, Colorado.

The French Company has also interested prospective government clients in upwards of a dozen countries around the world.

What Do You Think? _____

1. Would you be willing to travel on this type of train? Why or why not?
2. What might some of the disadvantages of such trains be? The advantages?

---

5. Let's Ban Autos*

Far more revolutionary than rapid transit are proposals to ban large automobiles entirely from downtown streets. A San Diego city planner envisions one way in which this could be done.

San Francisco Examiner, February 6, 1974.

With luck and a little help from the federal government, the automobile could be extinct in downtown San Diego within five years, a city planner says.

In its place could be electric-powered one-car "people movers," rolling quietly above the city at 30 miles an hour on elevated tracks, linking peripheral parking garages with any downtown street corner in five minutes. City streets, meanwhile, would be for pedestrians only.

The system, known as MAC for "Major Activity Center," is running in embryonic form at a West Virginia college campus, and is in the planning stage in half a dozen cities, says Andrew P. Schlaefli, supervising transportation planner in the San Diego Planning Department.

"People will tell you regional mass transit is the only answer," he said. "Well, a mass transit system like San Francisco is now getting takes about 20 years to build. We just finished a study that says it will be impossible to bring any more autos into San Diego center city in another ten years.

"The freeway is the weak link. Each freeway lane can carry 2000 cars in an hour. There's no way to get any more in. With the city's plans to redevelop the downtown area and just about double the number of people here each day, even with metered lanes, car pools and staggered work shifts we could not accommodate the automobile physically."

One of the most appealing aspects of the MAC system is that passengers might ride free, Schlaefli said.

"Because the streets would be closed to cars, maybe there would be enough advantage to developers to pay the local cost of the system," he said. "If not, it could be paid for out of the gasoline tax, as the police and fire department are paid for by taxes."

What Do You Think? _____

How feasible is a solution such as this?

---

6. Alternatives to the Automobile

Businesses in the United States have been responding to the demand for new forms of transportation for our cities. The three articles which follow give some idea of the wide range of response across the world. Would they be accepted in your area?

Big Plans in Brazil for a Little Electric Car*

A Brazilian firm has designed an electric car that will cost only one-eighth as much to run as a small gasoline-powered car and will begin production this year.

The first cars will cruise at a little over 30 mph and will have a range of

San Francisco Chronicle, February 6, 1973, p. 34.

60 miles, but the firm's engineers say they are confident they will soon be able to extend this.

The firm is Gurgel Industria e Commercio de Vehiculos, Ltda., which has built up a solid reputation in the past few years with specialist adaptations of standard cars, especially the Brazilian-made Volkswagen. Its products include sports cars, dune buggies and a rugged go-anywhere car called the Xavante.

The car and its engine are completely Brazilian products. They have been developed by Gurgel in cooperation with two other Brazilian firms.

It will be powered by a special lead-acid battery. Present batteries weigh nearly 300 pounds, but in order to extend the range, engineers expect that the battery will weigh about 350 pounds when the car goes on the market.

Barreiros admitted that the weight of the battery had been a problem in producing a light car, but he added that Gurgel had overcome it by producing a vehicle with a strong but light metal frame and then constructing the body-work of plastic and fiberglass.

The electric car is square-looking, but comfortable with good head and leg room and huge, flat windows giving excellent visibility. It has seats for a driver and one passenger and a large flat space behind the seats for luggage.

In the area of greater Sao Paulo, which has an air pollution problem ranking among the worst in the world, the promise of a silent, non-polluting car has raised considerable interest.

The city administration of Rio Claro has agreed to cooperate in the first practical street tests by allowing the Gurgel electric to park free in certain parts of the downtown area while the batteries are being recharged.

Gurgel is hoping other cities will follow Rio Claro's lead. The electric cars can be recharged at the home of the owner, but if there are facilities to recharge the batteries while the cars are parked in town it will obviously increase their usefulness.

Rio Claro will install special charging points at parking lots and the electricity authority of the state of Sao Paulo is considering supplying power free of charge in the beginning to encourage development and sales.

Gasoline Scarce? Why Not Try a Taiwanese Pedicab*

An enterprising Taiwanese firm is seeking to export its own practical solution to the world gasoline scarcity.

The Pedicab Service Center of Taipei has mailed out a one-page catalogue picturing eight of its current models—all modernized versions of the ancient "rickshaw."

Most of them are mounted on a foot-pedaled bicycle chassis. There are two with small gasoline engines.

Prices for the foot-pedaled models range from about $400 (including delivery costs to the U.S.) to a high of about $1000 for an enclosed-van type called "the Kindergarten Shuttle."

*Reprinted by permission from *The Christian Science Monitor,* February 15, 1974. Copyright © 1974. The Christian Science Publishing Society. All rights reserved.

They're all called "pedicabs"—a vehicle common in Southeast Asia, but until now thought to be on the way out.

The Taiwan firm is apparently basing its hopes for a revival not only on the gasoline shortage, but on a variety of models with novel features that may appeal to prospective customers in the West.

Almost all the models are "convertibles" with collapsible tops that can be put down for enjoying more of the weather or the countryside.

Most have the "driver" in front, giving him the best view of the road and his passengers maximum privacy.

But for those who want that up-front feeling for themselves—who like to ride the very prow of the ship—there's one model arranged that way, too.

This is the V9F model, popular among professionals in places like Jakarta. It's the equivalent of the rear-engined auto, putting the pedaler in the "push" position behind the passenger cab.

Some people say this is also the most "democratic" version, because it puts the pedaler close to the passenger's ear—permitting breezy conversation between them.

But for the greatest safety and comfort, other connoisseurs still prefer the more traditional horse-and-buggy style. It may put a damper on the pedaler's loquacity, but eases his steering considerably.

This is the standard arrangement, and it comes in several variations—plain, fancy, and ostentatious.

It also comes compact—a half-size, lightweight children's model for the elementary-school set.

This is not to be confused with the earlier mentioned "Kindergarten Shuttle," a heavy, strictly utilitarian model designed for transporting youngsters, but not for them to pedal themselves. Its buslike passenger module will hold half a dozen or more tots, depending upon their size, and will take strong feet at the pedals to get it rolling.

The ultimate, the limousine of the lot, is the "Palace Sedan" model. It has a fringed canopy, bas-relief dragons, disc wheels and other decorative features that are hard to describe.

But beneath them all is the heart and chassis of the common pedicab. Willing legs and a few drops of oil will keep them running for years. Taiwan is looking hopefully at the inscrutable American market.

Toronto Plan: Mass Transit, Pedestrian Malls, Car Maze*

Another imaginative plan has been proposed for Toronto, Canada. This proposal goes beyond that developed for San Diego, but there are basic similarities in both. Can you identify them?

A new plan for transportation in Toronto including "everything but magic carpets" as an alternative to cars in the city has been proposed.

*Reprinted by permission from *The Christian Science Monitor,* February 22, 1974. Copyright ©
71

A report from a task force of politicians, businessmen, and citizens groups, the plan seems likely to create a series of controversies because it recommends scrapping all conventional wisdom about city transportation.

Some suggestions include:

- The takeover of the city's private taxi industry by the city council and its transport commission to provide pools of taxis for passengers and goods, controlled by computer.
- Free rides on public transport for the hour before and after the morning and evening rush hour, to reduce congestion and as a first step to the long-term goal of totally free public transportation.
- The creation of pedestrian malls in the downtown area to create a maze through which cars would have to pass. Besides the intentional inconvenience to motorists, they would have to pay a fee of from $5 to $10 to enter.
- The replacement of all single-level parking lots by tiered structures. Only essential vehicles and pooled cars would be allowed to use them. Most parking lots would then become low-rise housing projects or parks.

On the whole, the report suggests a complete rezoning of the city to make larger areas of the center available for residential instead of office use.

It would, theoretically, make the downtown area move lively and allow people to walk to work, relieving strain on commuter traffic. It would generally reduce the cost of private housing, the report concluded.

The task force represented groups as diverse as the trucking and taxi industries and anti-pollution and neighborhood-preservation organizations.

The task force concluded that one-way streets should be abolished because they only encourage more wheeled traffic by speeding up the flow.

In its place they recommended setting up barricades to halt traffic passing through residential areas at all. One such system was recently set up in a Toronto suburb and provoked a major controversy.

The row developed over two concepts of "freedom"—the freedom of all taxpayers to drive over all roads in the city and the freedom of residents to protect their neighborhood against motorists who use it as a short cut, turning it into a freeway in the rush hours.

The general manager of the Toronto Transport Commission, James Kearns, commented on the report: "It seems to include everything but flying carpets."

What Do You Think? _____

1. The electric car has very limited range and speed. What value would it have in large cities?
2. The "Toronto Plan" is very comprehensive. Toronto has a relatively new subway system also. Could this program be adopted in other areas? Why or why not?
3. Which of these suggestions would you say has the most potential? the least? Why?

7. A Traffic Jam—In The Air!*

While there are problems in our ability to go short distances, we also have transportation difficulties with longer trips. Does this sound familiar?

A Monday morning in October, unseasonably warm, visibility excellent. No apparent reason why the gleaming jet at Newark Airport cannot take off on schedule for Washington.

A passenger seated in the handsome new DC-9-30, one of a fleet which Eastern Air Lines has just bought for its intercity shuttle service, picks some literature out of the seat pocket in front of him.

He reads that the DC-9-30 is capable of flying 520 m.p.h. His schedule, however, says that takeoff time is 8:30, and landing time is 9:20. Why so long to fly 250 miles? The passenger, through long experience, knows that the airline must allow extra time for taxiing, clearing the field, takeoff, and possible delays.

Even so, Eastern has been optimistic. Monday mornings are exceptionally busy. Air traffic backs up on the ground and overhead. The captain's voice crackles over the intercom. He apologizes, says there will be "a few minutes delay." Minutes tick on. An hour goes past before the craft roars down the runway for takeoff.

With its 520 m.p.h. capacity, the jet can make up some of the lost time. But not an hour's worth.

Problem Called Crisis

The passenger fidgets, grumbles, then settles back resignedly. He has an 11 o'clock appointment in Washington, but based on past experience, he has allowed for such a delay. Soon the plane banks into a turn over National Airport.

The captain's voice again. More apologies. Traffic has backed up. The jet must go into the stack for another "few minutes." The passenger squirms, glances anxiously at his watch. Twenty minutes later the plane settled into its landing glide.

It is 10:30 when the passenger bolts from the plane, through the terminal, and grabs a cab. He is just in time for his appointment.

This incident, repeated countless times over, is the red flag that should warn the flying public of impending trouble. Like the top of an iceberg, airline delays are only the visible top 10 per cent of a mountain of problems. Lumped together they add up to what [former] Secretary of Transportation Alan S. Boyd terms a national airport crisis: Among these troubles:

- Increasing congestion in the air over and around major commercial airports and with this congestion, increasing difficulty in maintaining minimum safety margins.
- Increasing congestion on the ground. This includes congestion of planes on runways, taxiing strips, and aprons. It also involves overtaxed parking, terminal, ticketing, baggage, and other passenger facilities.
- The chronic and worsening problem of moving passengers between airports and city centers.
- Increasing levels of aircraft noise over residential areas around airports.
- A growing load on the already overtaxed personnel who man air-control facilities at airport towers and regional centers.
- Mounting opposition to the freedom of general aviation—a catch-all category that covers everything from a Piper Cub to a 10-passenger corporation-owned jet—to use the facilities of major commercial airports.
- The constant preoccupation of airlines, airport operators and governments at all levels with the problem of getting money to pay for urgently needed new facilities.

---

8. Some Suggested Solutions*

Technological developments suggest ways of easing our air transport problems. Here are some of those developments.

Somewhere in the wilds of Malaya, a squat plane flits across the treetops and suddenly dips to a quick, short landing in what appears to be a mere patch of grass amidst the trees.

An observer unacquainted with short takeoff and landing (STOL) planes like the five passenger Helio Courier, might think that the little single-engined craft had crashed into the trees at the other end of the clearing, for lack of runway.

But STOL planes have been making such tight-squeeze landings for years. They have served bush pilots, missionaries, and combat troops in jungle wars. . . .

Along with the VTOLs (vertical takeoff and landing craft) more familiarly known as helicopters, STOLs are one of the more promising solutions to the problem of air congestion in the United States.

Right now, of course, helicopters are being used in major cities around the country to transport air travelers—those prepared to pay the price—from city centers to nearby airports.

*George H. Favre, "Quick Takeoff Planes Hold City-to-City Transportation Hope." Reprinted by permission from *The Christian Science Monitor.* Copyright © 1968. The Christian Science Publishing Society. All rights reserved.

Busy Corridor

But the new frontier in commercial aviation is the short haul from city center to city center—bypassing the major airports completely and using landing pads (for VTOLs) or short runways from 300 to 1,500 feet (for STOLs).

Take the Northeast corridor, for example. Within a 500 mile coastal strip are such major cities as Boston, New York, Philadelphia, Baltimore, and Washington. Together they have the heaviest air traffic of any corridor in the nation. In fact, one-third of all the domestic air traffic going out of New York goes to one of the other four cities.

If a workable short haul, low flying air system could be built in under the high flying system serving major cities, it would cut back air congestion tremendously. Such a cutback would add years of potential expansion to the rapidly clogging Northeast corridor's major airports.

If all goes well, this could come about, say experts, within a decade. Ideally, it would have been developed by now. But progress has been halting. Research and progress development on V/STOL planes . . . large enough to do the job has not yet broken through technical difficulties. A workable system needs planes capable of carrying from 50 to 120 passengers.

One promising design is the 56 passenger French Breguet 941, a four engined STOL craft that cruises at 285 mph. It is still in the testing stage. Some American STOL models are also in the works.

Most experts favor STOLs over VTOLs for an intercity system. Their obvious drawback is that they require more landing room.

Available Space

STOLs, with their need for 300 to 1,500 feet of runway, have their own obvious drawbacks in the downtown area of cities where land costs may run $40 or $60 or more a square foot. But that problem is not insoluble.

Both the scheduled airlines and the cities which may be served by a shorthaul intercity system are already thinking in terms of where to put "STOLports" and how to regulate their use.

Depending on the city and its particular needs and potentials there is a wide range of possible STOLport sites. In a land scarce, heavily congested area like New York, with waterfront space, an obvious answer is to use man-made islands or docks in the water. Airspace over railroad yards is another possibility. Rooftops, like the Pan Am Building, offer a solution where the noise problem does not raise insurmountable problems for City Hall.

Farther out at the edge of the city, shopping plaza, industrial parks, and highways are further possible STOLport sites.

* * * * *

Samuel J. Solomon, a patriarchal innovator of the aviation field, has just patented plans for a combination office, transportation center, parking and hotel complex whose common roof would form a V/STOLport. Mr. Solomon visualizes it in a decaying section of Washington or New York. It would sound like pie in the sky, except for the fact that Mr. Solomon has been doing this kind of thing throughout his aviation career.

Founder and president of several airlines at various times, including Northeast, the originator of helicopter passenger and mail feeder service, and former manager of Washington National Airport, he has a proven practical head for air service innovation.

A study by the Center for Transportation Studies at Eagleton Institute, part of Rutgers University in New Brunswick, N.J., came up with the "aquadromes" as an answer to the STOLport situation in New York. These would be saucer-shaped floating islands, anchored in the river, and would cost from $5 to $10 million each.

Whatever shape such STOLports may eventually take, and whoever may build and operate them, the commercial airlines are moving ahead on the premise that short haul intercity air service is their next frontier of major expansion. . . .

Some crucial questions remain. One of the hardest is what safety standards must be set for new-design planes. One example is the compound helicopter—reminiscent of the Autogiro—which combines wings and forward propulsion engines with the familiar "chopper" blades that give vertical flight. When such craft make the transition from fast forward flight to slow speed approach and hover flight, what performance characteristics are acceptable? No one knows for sure, as yet, nor will they until actual prototypes are flown and tested.

What Do You Think? _____

1. How does the development of STOLs and VTOLs help solve the problems raised in Reading 8? Do you think the low-flying system will work?
2. It is possible that new types of planes will bring about more growth in the suburbs and extend the suburbs to greater distances from the central city. Would this development solve the air transport problem of cities in the United States? Explain.

ACTIVITIES FOR INVOLVEMENT

1. Invite a member of an automobile dealers association to come to class to talk about the views of the dealers and producers relative to freeways and the expansion of automobile use.
2. Arrange a field trip to the air control center at the local airport. At the same time, talk with some pilots and an airline company representative. Check the viewpoints of these people for agreements and disagreements.
3. Arrange a debate on the following question: Resolved: Federal funds for highways should be cut by one-half and spent on rapid transit systems serving the major metropolitan areas.

4. Form a transportation committee to develop a proposal that will allow passengers to get from downtown to the airport in 40 minutes. Have the committee illustrate its proposal with appropriate maps, charts, and sketches.

5. Conduct a survey among a random sample of students as to whether or not they would ride a rapid transit system, and why. Tally the results as well as the reasons they offer pro and con. Now conduct a second survey among a random sample of adults in the community at large. Again tally the responses and reasons given. How do the two lists compare? Hold a class discussion on how to explain any differences and similarities noted.

6. Listed below are a number of actions that could be taken to deal with the problem of air congestion.
   - The number of people flying could be limited to those who have important business.
   - Certain days of the week could be closed to all air traffic except major airlines.
   - People living near airports could be moved.
   - Very strict regulations on air traffic could be adopted.
   - Certain hours of every day could be prohibited to *any* air traffic.
   - Larger aircraft could be developed.
   - Airlines could be restricted as to the *number* of flights they could offer per day.
   - People could be paid *not* to fly, but to travel by some other means of transportation.
   - The federal government could offer subsidies to railroads to improve their service.

   Rank these suggestions as to their feasibility. Then write a brief paper (two pages maximum) as to which you think offers the most and which the least promise—and why.

7. Transportation planners say we need a "mix" of transportation systems in an area to make an effective overall system. Expand your transportation committee proposal to include a total transportation system for your community. Present this plan to your city council.

5
POLLUTION:
OUR POISONED
ENVIRONMENT

Life seemingly holds more excitement for more people than ever before in history. Yet the very air we breathe presents a major problem to man. And the waters we depend upon for drinking, for agriculture, and for recreation are clouded with pollutants which can cause incalculable harm.

Air and water pollution are but two aspects of the tremendous challenge imposed by our mass production and mass consumption way of life. Another is the disposal of waste—garbage, old cars, and other discards from our prolific technology. By virtue of sheer productivity, we are faced with a crisis in our environment.

Like many of the problems of modern man, air pollution is not particularly new. King Edward I of England set forth a law limiting the burning of coal in 1273. Since that time, there have been numerous attempts to clean up the air. London, Germany, Chicago, and California are just some of the places where law-making bodies have attempted to control the quality of air breathed by their citizens. The U.S. federal government has also developed an air pollution control system.

Air can become polluted by foreign matter from camp fires, burning trash, industrial waste, automobile exhaust fumes, or atomic waste matter. Each improvement in technology seems to create new problems of waste disposal. Currently, the increase in the numbers of automobiles is causing great concern. Along with this growth has come an alarming increase in the incidence of lung cancer.

The evidence is indisputable: polluted air can cause illness and death. The damage can be done quickly or over a long period of time. In 1948 in Donora, Pennsylvania, 18 people died and thousands more were made ill by waste matter that persisted in the air for several days. In London, England, in 1952, smoke, soot, and fog hung over the city for a week. In that time over 4,000 deaths were attributed to the aerial wastes, and many more lives were shortened by resultant illnesses.

Medical people generally agree that there is strong evidence that air pollution is associated with a number of respiratory ailments. These include (1) nonspecific infectious upper respiratory disease, (2) chronic bronchitis, (3) chronic constrictive ventilatory disease, (4) pulmonary emphysema, (5) bronchial asthma, and (6) lung cancer. On the state and local level, authorities are also concerned about the menace. Strong programs have been adopted in Pittsburgh, Pennsylvania; St. Louis, Missouri; and Los Angeles, California. The state government in California has established controls on automobile exhausts which are stronger than federal controls passed in 1967.

In recent years, as the nation has become more concerned with energy and the seeming need to switch from oil to coal as a source of industrial power, there has been increasing pressure to relax clean-air laws passed during the 1960s. This pressure has resulted in proposals for change from both the Congress and the President. Are Americans willing to pay for clean air with lower production and a possible lower standard of consumption of material goods?

Paying for control can be done through tax-supported efforts, as in Los Angeles and San Francisco, or it can be done by forcing the owner-offender to provide for safe elimination of wastes. Either way, the individual citizen will ultimately pay the bill, for the factory or utility owner will pass on his increased costs in the form of higher prices. In the final analysis, it is the average citizen who must decide for himself how much clean air is worth.

In some areas water pollution is a critical problem. The Ohio River Valley Sanitation Commission, formed by eight states in 1948, has had some success in cleaning up this once beautiful river. Before the formation of the commission, over 1,000 cities had been dumping raw sewage into the Ohio. There are still problems to be overcome before the river is returned to its former condition. Lake Erie illustrates a similar problem, as does the Lake Tahoe area between California and Nevada.

Water pollution is linked to the inadequate systems of sewers in our cities, but this is only a part of the problem. Industrial waste accounts for at least as much of our water pollution. Water is used in great quantities in many industrial processes and is then returned, loaded with wastes, to streams, rivers, or lakes.

Even new farming techniques provide a source of water pollution. Since the invention of DDT in the early 1940s, many new chemical compounds have been discovered which control harmful insects but which in turn may be harmful to man or wildlife. The use of chemical fertilizers appears to result in an increase in the algae found in waters receiving such chemicals, a process still little understood.

Atomic waste materials may be an important future source of pollution. At present such waste is buried or dumped sealed in concrete containers in the oceans. As the world increases its use of atomic power, the amount of such waste will greatly increase. New methods of disposal will have to be found.

The problems imposed by pollution of the environment are very difficult. Often people prefer not to act until the situation becomes an obvious threat. This can be too late. Our increasing population and our increasingly technological society are going to create more and more waste matter. Somehow, this waste must be disposed of if it is not to prove a serious menace to man and to the good life he wishes to lead.

1. Pollution Is No New Problem*

Pollution and concern for the quality of life have been written and talked about for many years. Here is poet James Thomson's view of the city. How would you describe this view?

What men are they who haunt these fatal glooms
And fill their living mouths with dust to death,
And make their habitations in the tombs,
And breathe eternal sighs with mortal breath,
And pierce life's pleasant veil of various error
To reach that void of darkness and old terror
Wherein expire the lamps of hope and faith?
Unspoken passion, wordless meditation,
Are breathed into it with our respiration
It is with our life fraught and overfraught.

So that no man there breathes earth's simple breath,
As if alone on mountains or wide seas;
But nourishes warm life or hastens death
With joys and sorrows, health and foul disease,
Wisdom and folly, good and evil labours
Incessant of his multitudinous neighbors;
He in his turn affecting all of these.

That City's atmosphere is dark and dense,
Although not many exiles wander there,
With many a potent evil influence,
Each adding poison to the poisoned air
Infections of unutterable sadness
Infections of incalculable madness,
Infections of incurable despair.

They have much wisdom yet they are not wise,
They have much goodness yet they do not well,
(The fools we know have their own Paradise,
The wicked also have their proper Hell):
They have much strength but still their doom is stronger,
Much patience but their time endureth longer
Much valor but life mocks it with some spell.

---

*Excerpted from "The City of Dreadful Night," (1874), by the nineteenth century British poet James Thomson, better known as "B.V."

They are most rational and yet insane:
An outward madness not to be controlled;
A perfect reason in the central brain,
Which has no power, but sittest wan and cold.
And sees the madness, and foresees as plainly
The ruin in its path, and trieth vainly
To cheat itself refusing to be bold.

And some are great in rank and wealth and power,
And some renowned for genius and for worth;
And some are poor and mean, who brook and cower
And shrink from notice, and accept all dearth
Of body, heart and soul, and leave to others
All boons of life; yet these and those are brothers,
The saddest and the weariest men on earth.

Wherever men are gathered, all the air
Is charged with human feeling, human thought;
Each shout and cry and laugh, each curse and prayer,
Are into its vibrations surely wrought. . . .

What Do You Think?

1. In your own words, describe the city as Thomson sees it. Is he referring to a real city? What else might he be referring to?
2. Suppose you were asked to respond to Thomson. What would you say?

---

2. The Effects of Smog*

Smog looks bad, but does it really do any harm? While medical people disagree as to the total effects of smog on human beings, it is generally agreed that it is unhealthy. Los Angeles suffers from heavy smog during many days of the year. What about your community?

The medical evidence is compelling. Writing in the November 1970 *California Medicine,* Dr. John Goldsmith, head of the environmental unit of the California Department of Public Health, estimated the damage caused by photochemical air pollution in the Los Angeles Basin:
"Excess mortality, 100 to 500 persons per year
Aggravation of disease, 50,000 to 500,000
Impairment of function, 100,000 to 2.5 million
Interference with well-being, 9.3 million"

*Reprinted with permission from "Stop Driving or Stop Breathing," by Gil Bailey, in the Fall 1973 issue of *Cry California,* published by California Tomorrow, San Francisco.

"I can remember this neighborhood before it became uninhabitable."

Dr. Gerald A. Heidbreder, Los Angeles County Health Officer, noted in 1971 that the number of fatalities from emphysema, lung cancer and chronic bronchitis had more than doubled in the Los Angeles Basin. Dr. Goldsmith cited additional studies which showed "excess deaths" among heart patients when auto-produced carbon-monoxide pollution increases.

Dr. Hurley L. Motley, a respiratory expert, speaking as chairman of the Scientific Advisory Committee to the Los Angeles Air Pollution Control District, estimated that between ten and 15 percent of the ten million people in the Los Angeles Basin suffer directly from the effects of air pollution—between one million and 1.5 million people.

"In an area such as the Los Angeles Basin, the air supply is limited," said Dr. Motley. "The air supply appears to be a more limiting factor for future growth in Los Angeles County . . . [than] the water supply. Population growth results in more people, more cars and more pollution."

The Environmental Protection Agency (EPA) based its safe air standards on the health effects of smog. "Impairment of performance by high-school athletes has been observed when photochemical oxidants exceeded .07 ppm (parts per million parts of air) for one hour immediately prior to the start of **83** activity," an EPA health study reported. "Eye irritation under conditions prevalent in Los Angeles is likely to occur in a large fraction of the population when oxidant concentrations in ambient[1] air increase to .10 ppm." In addition, the studies pointed out, asthma is likely to be aggravated at .13 ppm, while vegetation is damaged at .05 ppm. EPA set the health standard for air at .08 ppm, not to be exceeded more than once a year.

In 1970, according to the figures of the Los Angeles County Air Pollution Control District, the federal health standards were violated on at least 264 days. Much higher smog levels—.40 ppm and .60 ppm—were recorded in the years 1970, 1971, 1972, and 1973.

What Do You Think?

1. Transportation experts tell us we need to develop new transportation systems. Does the issue of smog and pollution control help or hurt their case?
2. Why do people put up with smog anyway?

---

3. One Proposal to Deal with the Problem*

Los Angeles has long been noted for smog attacks—periods of time when air pollution reaches dangerous or uncomfortable levels. A 1973 proposal to cut smog created a storm of protest. It was later abandoned as being impractical. Was such abandonment a wise decision?

At a crowded Los Angeles press conference on January 15, 1973, William Ruckelshaus, the highly personable former administrator of the federal Environmental Protection Agency (EPA), proposed the only realistic solution yet offered to the problem of dangerous concentrations of smog in the Los Angeles Basin. He acted only because a federal court had told him to enforce the law requiring healthy air for all Americans, even those living in Los Angeles. Ruckelshaus suggested the unthinkable—gasoline rationing—to cut the vehicle-miles traveled in the basin, thus sharply reducing the number of tons of pollutants discharged into the air.

Fundamentally, gasoline rationing could work. If it were enforced, Los Angeles residents would have cleaner skies and more than a million people now suffering health damage from smog would be helped. With any committment to act decisively, staggered work hours, car pools, bus transit and other measures could quickly be implemented.

The rationing proposal, radical as it may seem, is essential to the health

[1]Surrounding.
*Reprinted with permission, from "Stop Driving or Stop Breathing," by Gil Bailey, in the Fall 1973 issue of *Cry California,* published by California Tomorrow, San Francisco.

of the ten million residents of the Los Angeles Basin. A review of the geography, history and politics of the basin in regard to air pollution shows clearly that only such a basic step, enforced by the federal government, can control traffic congestion and air pollution.

Ruckelshaus' plan drew an immediate and fierce outcry from federal, state and local officials. "The EPA rationing proposal would be an administrative nightmare unless, of course, it (EPA) would be willing to call in the national guard," said Senator John Tunney, who then trotted out his own multibillion-dollar program to build a smog-free automobile engine within three years. Local officials also joined in the protest. Former Los Angeles Mayor Sam Yorty, who despite his long tenure in office may not have stayed in town long enough at any given time to notice the smog, called the idea "shocking" and "economy-destroying." Newly elected Los Angeles County Supervisor James Hayes, who is in charge of the Los Angeles County Air Pollution Control District, said the proposal was "unrealistic" and "unnecessary."

In June the EPA, still in disarray after Ruckelshaus' sudden departure to become director of the FBI, modified the proposal, dropping its suggested 80-percent-plus gasoline rationing during high smog months. The concession was not enough for county officials. The idea of a limit on gasoline supplies, parking restrictions, establishment of bus and car-pool lanes, and vehicle inspection was too much for those same officials.

Supervisor Hayes commented, "Why doesn't EPA jump on the auto manufacturers instead of imposing a drastic economic penalty on working men and women, is the big unanswered question." Hayes, of course, ignored continuing efforts of EPA to impose effective auto-emission controls on the industry, controls which have brought angry protests from the manufacturers.

Supervisor Kenneth Hahn joined the attack on EPA, saying the modified plan was "ridiculous." He added, "Limiting the automobile will paralyze our communities." Hahn noted accurately that Los Angeles does not have a rapid-transit system, but ignored the responsibility of the board of supervisors for the lack of such a system and for the growing smog crisis.

Newly elected Mayor Thomas Bradley, acting more calmly, flew to Washington, D.C., in an effort to obtain funds for an improved rapid-transit system. Hayes joined in that effort, achieving at least one victory for the EPA proposals as, for the first time in recent history, local officials began to consider seriously other means of transportation than the auto.

What Do You Think?

1. Why do you suppose people reacted so strongly against the idea of gas rationing?

2. Is the auto industry likely to develop auto emission-control devices without government prodding? Why or why not?

3. One proposal for large cities is to ban all automobiles from the downtown area during certain hours. Would this help deal with smog? Is it feasible?

4. Cartoonists Comment

Here are some thoughts about the causes of pollution in cartoon form. What is the point of each?

"THAT'S NOT AN ENEMY ATTACK, CHILDREN—THOSE ARE FRIENDLY FELLOW-AMERICANS."

"It can't be sundown, so it must be air pollution."

What Do You Think?

Are cartoons more or less likely than articles and editorials to alert people to the dangers of pollution? Explain. What about moving them to action?

5. A Way to Help*

It is possible for high school teachers and students to do something about pollution, as the following story indicates.

Ohio's 813-square-mile Cuyahoga River watershed has become both a battlefield and a laboratory for a small band of teachers and students determined to fight environmental deterioration on its own grounds.

At 12 sites that appear as bright spots of hope on a dark map of the polluted river basin, they are beating drums along the Cuyahoga—from its headwaters in Hambden Township to its entrance into Lake Erie at Cleveland —calling for communities to hold against environmental damage which has mounted persistently since the early 1800's when the Senecas, Ottawas, Delawares, and Chippewas began falling back before the inexorable advance of industrialization that powered through the forest of the Western Reserve. Teacher-student teams, trained by environmental education specialists of the Cleveland-based nonprofit Institute for Environmental Education, conduct environmental studies in public school systems. . . .

The meandering 103-mile-long Cuyahoga, befouled in one place or another by almost all of man's wastes, provides an unparalleled laboratory for exploring fundamental, practical aspects of the environment in terms that every student can understand. Boys and girls in the eighth grade at St. Patrick's Elementary, for example, go down to the banks of the Cuyahoga and its tributaries, bottle some water, take it back to school, and analyze it in their science classroom. The students are shown how to discover pollutants by using a portable chemical and filtering set about the size of a trombone case, supplied by IEE. Drops from the water samples are also examined under a microscope. Magnification frequently reveals coliform bacteria, the presence of which, students learn, indicates fecal pollution. Students are called upon to submit written reports of their investigations, and a basic finding is that the waste-treatment facilities of the communities involved lack the capacity to handle the situation. And there is a common message: The job of cleaning up the water cannot be postponed.

---

*W. Wood, "Ecological Drums Along the Cuyahoga," *American Education,* January-February 1973.

The procedure at St. Patrick's is one of several parts of the overall program—officially known as the Cuyahoga River Watershed Project—funded for three years by USOE under the Environmental Education Act.

In a class in earth science at Davey Junior High in Kent, a girl has a plastic cylinder with soil dug from her own back yard. One of her classmates has a similar cylinder with soil from his yard. Both students add distilled water to their containers, tilt them to get rid of the air bubbles, and watch to see whose soil retains the most water. At other tables in the lab, other students are determining the weight of soil samples in grams on a chemical balance or measuring the amount of water seeping through selected kinds of soils. The key question in these analyses—and in contributing to an understanding of the overall status of the local environment—is the degree of permeability.[1] The students have by now brought in soil samples from property throughout the environs of Kent—with what their teacher, Jim Henry, sees as two valuable results: City officials now have a head start in determining the location of the most suitable soil strata on which to erect the town's proposed new sewage treatment plant; and the students have learned an indelible lesson in the practical relationship between the local environment and local community needs.

Each teacher in the training program was required to bring a student to work with, to learn and teach together. The teacher-student teams trekked across the watershed, studying problems related to water and air pollution, erosion and siltation,[2] solid wastes disposal, land use, and map interpretation. At a special lab set up in the Cleveland Health Museum and Education Center they evaluated water samplings for criteria, including soil and sediment content, macroinvertebrates, and chemical variables. Hurricane Agnes was an unexpected contributor to the studies, giving teachers and students a rare

---

[1]The rate in which fluid can go through the soil.

[2]Filling up with sandy material, or silt.

opportunity to observe the Cuyahoga Valley in one of its worst flood conditions.

Two students from Davey Junior High completed the four weeks of summer training with Henry and are now helping him teach earth science. Qualified high school juniors and seniors can ultimately receive undergraduate credit at Cleveland State for their work on the teams. The teams have generally come to the conclusion that the Cuyahoga project should be seen first as an instrument for creating practical understanding of environmental problems, and then as a process for bringing about instant change—though change is of course the essential goal. So they are concentrating now on developing effective teaching methods and materials and on evaluating their growth as the project proceeds.

"Mistakes will probably be made, but that's what learning is all about," says Henry. "We want to look at the problem and figure out how to attack it." . . .

The structure of the curriculums being developed in the Cuyahoga project epitomize IEE Vice President Offutt's belief that "environmental education cannot be imposed; it must be experienced."

The Cuyahoga teachers and students beating the drums for a better environment are only a small band now, but the hope is that the cadre will be a battalion tomorrow and perhaps one day an army—moving far beyond that river to encompass similarly afflicted watersheds throughout the Nation.

What Do You Think?

Schools have been criticized as being "irrelevant." Is the IEE program "relevant"? Why or why not?

6. Scientific Possibilities Offer Hope*

Scientists are even now devising new approaches which will cut down on the poisoning of our world. But is there time?

The founders of our cities regarded air and water the way the Indians did buffalo. There was always more where the last supply came from, and nature took away whatever people polluted. Smog and streams no longer safe to wade in have reminded our generation that nature's bounty is not infinite.

The city is a growing component of a global ecological system that we barely have begun to understand. Instruments in orbiting satellites will soon help environmental scientists detect, trace, and predict global trends. Changes

*Excerpted from *Science and the City,* U.S. Department of Housing and Urban Development.

may be accelerated at the same time by such projects as the American Water and Power Alliance's proposal to redistribute water throughout the North American continent. Whole cities may seem in a few more decades to have been badly placed.

Until the weather makers perfect their art, or we put cities under some kind of glass, nature will meter the input of air to them and handle the output in its whimsical ways. Yet we no longer need to contaminate the winds that blow through cities with such great volumes of foul gas from our vehicles, factories, and homes as we do now. It is no longer necessary to use fuel that gives off smoke and harmful fumes in densely populated places, or to let city dumps smolder day and night. By using electrical power and modern means of refuse disposal, we could lessen the city's pollution of the earth's atmosphere.

With modern technology we also could reduce the city's contamination of water. It enters and leaves the city through the umbilical cords designed and built by men. Chemical, mechanical, and civil engineers are capable now of improving many of both the input and the output lines in ways that would help the whole country get more use and pleasure from its water resources.

Municipal water and sewage systems, of course, are the responsibility of men intent on minimizing taxes. The demands placed on these systems, on the other hand, are determined by men intent on maximizing profits. Each group has given a little and taken a little from the other—but often has taken a little more than it gave. The result has been increasing extravagance with the earth's water.

Trash in the Kitchens

American engineers have built completely closed ecological systems for astronauts. They may have to for our grandchildren, too, if we do not amend some of our methods. We still have alternatives, luckily, such as changing our food-handling, temperature-governing and plumbing practices.

Although our refuse, garbage and other solid waste matter already total 800,000,000 pounds a day, we go right on lugging food into our kitchens in bottles and boxes that cannot be compacted or consumed when emptied. Such wrappings are overtaxing the trucks that haul our trash away. Why do we not tax the producers of nonreturnable, nondegradable containers instead of ourselves? They would quickly find substitutes, and we would not have to buy so many garbage trucks.

We heat and cool our homes with machinery we purchase with scarcely any regard for the amount of water they require. We use bathroom and kitchen appliances that send quantities of water down the drain so great they dismay cost conscious chemical engineers. Although utility and other big companies are spending millions to minimize their additions to pollutants in air and water, we are still paying little attention to the efficiency of things in our homes.

The electric garbage grinder under the kitchen sink in many new homes is an intriguing example of a convenience with side effects that the users tend to disregard. Some cities have forbidden its use because of its effects on their disposal systems; others have required its use, and some even have helped to pay for such grinders. Most of us, unfortunately, take the systems that bring and take things from urban homes for granted and pay scant heed to the problems that may be created elsewhere.

A city must be drained to prevent floods, but spring showers could be used to flush the streets in long hot summers if we kept some of the rainwater in rooftop or other reservoirs. When storm and sanitary sewers are conbined, the tubing must be large enough to carry great surges—but this is not the only possible way to reduce the danger of overflows of untreated sewage into family basements.

Chicago is considering a $100,000,000 test of an imaginative scheme to store storm water in tunnels 700 feet below the surface, use it to generate electric power, and lift it back to the surface for further use.

Environmental engineers have many ideas. It might be possible, for example, to treat sewage in the big pipes that carry it to discharge points more effectively than nature does after it reaches a river that carries the water to another city downstream. It also might be technically feasible and economically attractive to transport more of the solid matter out of the city in pipelines —and thus reduce the number of trucks disturbing our sleep by banging their way through the streets.

Utility Tunnels

A university campus is a microcosm of a city. There you often find utility tunnels between the buildings. All the pipes and wires needed to serve the occupants of several buildings go through these multi-purpose tunnels. This makes it easier to repair or replace any particular pipe or wire. If we had such tunnels under city streets, traffic would not be held up so often by men with signs saying "dig we must" (such as you see in Manhattan). Might not tunnels reduce our electric, telephone, gas, and other bills?

Alaskans call such big tubes "utilidors." They have made indoor plumbing reliable there, and cost benefit studies might show that they would be good investment in milder climates, too. It might pay, for example, to move some solid matter through vacuum tubing. Do we remove snow from our streets efficiently? Must vehicles in which people ride be delayed so much by men maneuvering and unloading long trucks? Could not many more things flow through pipes than do now?

What Do You Think? _____

There is a possible danger in relying on science to solve everything.

What could that danger be? Do you think it is actually a problem or merely something that might become a problem?

ACTIVITIES FOR INVOLVEMENT

1. Investigate the efforts being made by your community to control pollution. Arrange an interview with a local offical who knows about this problem, and get a list of the priorities established in your area for pollution control.

2. Send out a survey team to check any areas in your community which may be causing pollution. Prepare a report for the class in which you explain what you believe are the causes of any instances located, and then make a list of suggestions as to how the causes might be eliminated.

3. Ask someone from the automobile industry to talk about smog control and what is being done in Detroit to remedy this problem.

4. Call your local medical society and get its view on the health hazards of pollution in your area. If there is a problem, what should you do about it?

5. Try to write a poem of your own (review Reading 1 in this chapter) about your city, its virtues, and its defects.

6. Reread Reading 6. Take any one of the ideas suggested in the reading and examine it further. Prepare a brief research paper in which you describe your findings.

7. Have two members of the class role-play one of the following situations:
   - Two garbage collectors in New York discussing the food habits of people.
   - Two visitors from another planet visiting an American city during an evening traffic jam.
   - Two city dwellers in Los Angeles discussing the effects of smog.
   - A police officer giving an angry driver a ticket for speeding.
   - A farmer arguing against limiting the use of fertilizers.
   - Two secretaries complaining about riding to and from work on crowded city buses.

8. Write your local Representative in Congress and find out what the current federal guidelines are on pollution. Ask his or her position on this issue and what action is being taken.

9. Get a group to work with students in the science department to develop an antipollution policy for your city. Send your policy to the officials responsible for curbing pollution and ask them to comment.

6
THE
FUTURE
OF CITIES

The twenty-first century is almost upon us. All of us will be involved in making critical decisions for this nation well beyond the year 2000. Many of those decisions will inevitably have to do with the American city. In fact, the most challenging questions facing the nation may well be how we plan our cities, how we involve our citizens in the planning and in the life of the city, and how we use the technology we now have or may soon develop.

This is an age of planning. Or, more accurately, this is an age when many people talk about planning. It is easy to accept the idea that plans are necessary for orderly development. It is quite another matter to accept planning when these plans differ from your own conception of what is correct or interfere with your property rights or with some other aspect of your life.

Nevertheless, cities today have planning departments associated with the city government; large universities have departments in city and regional planning; and the demand for planners is increasing. As the population of the nation continues to rise and at the same time to concentrate in four or five large areas, there will be still greater concern over the quality of life being led by Americans. It is projected that by the year 2000 over 280 million Americans will be living in urban areas.

Herman Kahn and Anthony J. Wiener, writing in *Daedalus,*[1] identify three areas which they predict will hold roughly one-half of the population of the nation in the year 2000. They call these huge megalopolises "Boswash, Chipitts, and Sansan." Can you guess where they are?

Kahn and Wiener see "Boswash" as providing homes for close to 80 million people on the narrow Atlantic seacoast between Washington, D.C., and Boston. "Chipitts" will include those cities concentrated around the Great Lakes, and "Sansan" will stretch from Santa Barbara (or even San Francisco) to San Diego on the Pacific Coast.

Other predictors also mention the areas of Florida and Texas, where there is currently a population growth comparable to that of the three megalopolises above.

If these predictions are at all accurate, or even if they miss the mark by a considerable margin, it is easy to see why there is so much talk of planning today. There is no question that we have room for a much greater population; we need only look at the population density of Indonesia or England, for example, to see that the United States can hold many millions more people. What we must ask is this: (1) What kind of a nation do we wish to live in in the year 2000? (2) What are we willing to pay for that nation in terms of taxes and restraints on individual freedom?

The planners state that we can deliberately create a nation which will provide the good life for its citizens. We will live in a heavily populated world, but there need be little sense of crowding. There can be plenty of open space

[1]The Journal of the American Academy of Arts and Sciences. "Toward the Year 2000: Work in Progress," *Daedalus,* Summer 1967.

and recreational areas. Public transportation facilities can be available to all with little inconvenience or disruption of life. Air and water can be safe for all.

Those opposing planning argue that to implement such plans would require great restrictions on individual freedom. Their main concern is that the planners will eventually be telling everyone what to do and how to do it. This group also argues that the dreams of the planners are just that—dreams for which we cannot afford to pay. And, they also point out that planners make mistakes like anyone else.

Perhaps most people accept a position between the two extremes. They recognize the need for some kind of orderly growth within the nation and accept the fact that planning may be the tool by which it may be accomplished. At the same time they are wary as to the amount of power given to planners and anxious about the cost of recreating the American environment.

Planning is for people. New methods of involving the citizen in the planning process are gaining acceptance as are new technologies for construction, for cleaning the environment, and for communication. By intertwining the three ideas—planning, participation, and technology—it may be possible to transform the urban landscape and bring urban areas back to life.

Most of our cities were not planned from the start. They "just grew" for many years before there was a plan created for their growth. Rarely does a planner have the chance to begin from scratch—as was done, for example, in Reston, Virginia; Columbia, Maryland; or Irvine, California. Each of these is designed to be a comprehensive town in which individuals can work and live in comfort. Both Reston and Columbia are close to the nation's capital, and many people commute to Washington. Irvine has as its focal point one of the campuses of the University of California. It is expected that other planned communities will be created in the near future.

However, the planning of America's urban life will deal mainly with established cities and their suburbs. The various commissions, local political pressure groups, state legislatures, and others affected by the problems of urban-suburban living will have to hammer out solutions to the problems we face.

The following readings are designed to give some understanding of what the future may be like, and the problem and promise of planning, participation, and technology.

---

1. American Urban Areas—2000 A.D.*

The map and table which follow give some idea of what is predicted for America's urban areas by the year 2000.

*The Futurist, December 1972

By the Year 2000: Half of U.S. People May Live in Two Urban Regions

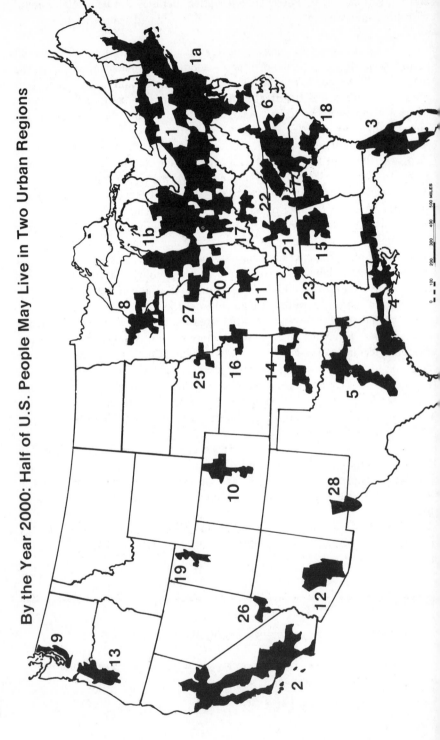

Urban Regions: Year 2000

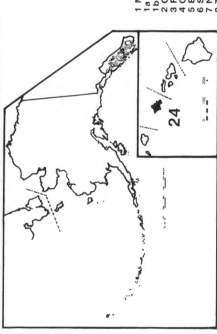

Urban regions with 10 million population or more by 2000.

Urban regions with 1-10 million population by 2000.

1 Metropolitan Belt
1a Atlantic Seaboard
1b Lower Great Lakes
2 California Region
3 Florida Peninsula
4 Gulf Coast
5 East Central Texas-Red River
6 Southern Piedmont
7 North Georgia-Southeast Tennessee
8 Twin Cities Region
9 Puget Sound
10 Colorado Piedmont
11 Saint Louis
12 Metropolitan Arizona
13 Willamette Valley

14 Central Oklahoma-Arkansas Valley
15 North Alabama
16 Missouri-Kaw Valley
17 Bluegrass
18 Southern Coastal Plain
19 Salt Lake Valley
20 Central Illinois
21 Nashville Region
22 East Tennessee
23 Memphis
24 Oahu Island
25 Platte Valley
26 Las Vegas
27 East Iowa-Mississippi Valley
28 El Paso-Ciudad Juarez (part)

*The Futurist, December 1972.

97

Two huge urban regions will contain more than half of the U.S. population in the year 2000, according to recent projections by urbanologist Jerome P. Pickard.

More than 40 percent of the people will live in a single super region—the Metropolitan Belt—which will extend from Illinois and Wisconsin eastward to Maine and Virginia. Another 13 percent will live in the California Urban Region, and nearly 5 percent in the Florida Peninsula Urban Region.

All told, the U.S. will have 28 urban regions with more than one million people apiece. Eight out of 10 Americans will live in them.

During the past 40 years, Pickard notes, the urban regions of the United States have grown explosively. If trends continue, by the year 2000 the land area of the urban regions will be 2.5 times as great as it was in 1960, and the total population will be 2.4 times as large.

Pickard's projections, prepared for the President's Commission on Population Growth and the American Future, are based on population growth in the period between 1940 and 1970.

Where We'll Live

This table shows U.S. urban regions that are projected to have one million or more people in the year 2000. (See map.) The projections were prepared by urban specialist Jerome P. Pickard for the President's Commission on Population Growth and the American Future. They are based on U.S. Census Bureau figures during past decades and on the Bureau's Series D projection for the birth rate, which is among the more conservative of several projections.

	Land Area in Thousands of Square Miles	Population in Millions		Population Density		Decennial Growth Rate	
		1970	2000	1970	2000	1970-1980	1980-2000
Total, 28 Urban Regions	502.9	155.9	239.9	310	477	16.4%	14.9%
Metropolitan Belt	180.1	85.9	117.7	477	653	11.5	10.8
Atlantic Seaboard	70.3	45.7	62.7	651	892	12.3	10.5
Lower Great Lakes	109.9	40.2	55.0	366	501	10.5	11.3
California Region	55.0	19.3	37.0	351	672	26.4	23.2
Florida Peninsula	22.2	5.9	13.5	265	610	38.2	29.0
Gulf Coast	29.7	5.8	9.9	195	332	22.1	18.2
E. Cent. Texas- Red River	23.4	4.6	7.9	197	337	22.2	18.3
Southern Piedmont	25.7	4.4	6.5	170	251	15.1	13.3
No. Georgia- SE. Tennessee	12.1	2.6	4.5	216	370	22.6	18.2
Twin Cities Region	16.2	2.8	3.9	170	244	15.2	11.6
Puget Sound	6.3	2.2	3.8	342	604	21.5	20.6
Colorado Piedmont	11.3	1.8	3.4	158	300	28.4	21.5
Saint Louis Metropolitan	5.4	2.4	3.2	451	599	10.9	9.4
Arizona	12.7	1.4	3.1	108	243	37.9	27.7

	Land Area in Thousands of Square Miles	Population in Millions		Population Density		Decennial Growth Rate	
		1970	2000	1970	2000	1970-1980	1980-2000
Willamette Valley	9.7	1.7	2.7	172	282	17.6	18.1
Cent. Oklahoma-Ark. Valley	15.0	1.8	2.5	118	170	15.0	12.0
North Alabama	13.1	1.8	2.3	134	175	10.9	8.4
Missouri-Kaw Valley	5.7	1.6	2.3	289	401	13.1	10.7
Bluegrass	5.4	1.4	2.1	256	389	16.7	14.1
Southern Coastal Plain	7.8	1.1	1.8	141	233	20.0	17.4
Salt Lake Valley	4.7	0.9	1.5	193	323	21.0	17.5
Central Illinois	7.7	1.1	1.4	142	179	8.5	7.8
Nashville Region	6.7	0.9	1.4	141	205	15.2	12.4
East Tennessee	7.1	1.0	1.3	141	180	9.3	8.0
Memphis	1.8	0.8	1.2	438	673	17.0	14.5
Oahu Island	0.6	0.6	1.1	1063	1902	23.9	20.1
Platte Valley	3.9	0.8	1.1	201	281	13.7	10.8
Las Vegas	4.6	0.3	1.0	59	223	70.9	48.7
East Iowa-Miss. Valley	5.4	0.8	1.0	142	189	11.2	9.3
El Paso-C. Juarez (part)	3.5	0.4	0.7	124	209	20.7	18.0
United States (including both urban and nonurban areas)	2970.4*	202.9*	286.3*	68*	96*	12.8%	11.8%

* Excludes Alaska.

2. The World City*

Planning is not an easy process. While all of us plan our lives to some degree, the planning of a city must take into account a great many elements—including people.

Suppose a city planner were a member of a group of astronauts preparing to land on an uninhabited—but habitable—planet. The planner's job: find sites for new cities. What would he look for?

Good drinking water, for one thing. A livable climate. Rivers, lakes, and roadbeds for surface transportation, perhaps a natural harbor. Level stretches of terrain for airfields. Within shipping distance, fertile fields for crops and grazing. Also within shipping distance: forests, minerals, other natural resources for use by industries. A way to dispose of sewage and garbage.

*"The World City," *Senior Scholastic,* December 4, 1972. Copyright © 1972 by Scholastic Magazines, Inc.

Nearly every big city on the planet Earth meets most of these requirements. But let one of these important factors drop down and out, and the city in question may end up by hitting the skids.

That's what did happen, in fact, to the ancient city of Ur in the equally ancient land of Sumer (now Iraq). Ur was founded about 3500 B.C. on a prime location along the Euphrates River. It might still be floushing today, except that the Euphrates changed its course. This left Ur sitting high and dry. Nowadays only the archaeologists poke around Ur.

But Ur in its time was a busy place. It was a market town where farmers brought their grains and fruits to sell. It was a trading center where goods made in Ur or shipped in from smaller towns were bought and sold. It was a manufacturing city where metal objects were made and precious stones were cut. It had merchants, craftsmen, builders, scribes, unskilled workers—and probably too many city officials. In short, much like a city of today.

Durable Centers

Other ancient cities have lasted into modern times, still going strong. Athens and Rome were thriving before the B.C.'s turned into the A.D.'s, and they remain important cities. But their ancient glories, under attack by urban pollution and just plain old age, need repair and restoration. The Colosseum in Rome, for example, is crumbling and requires a stem-to-stern renewal. Pisa's Leaning Tower may be leaning over too far.

London, England, came into existence shortly after the Romans conquered Britain in A.D. 43. It started as a tiny settlement called Londinium near the bridge across the River Thames. Today London proper has about eight million people, and Greater London—which includes the suburbs—has more than 12 million.

In its 2,000-year history, London has grown without plans or blueprints. Its streets zig, zag, snake, and circle. There's no reason or order to its street-numbering system. Indeed, no one but a veteran taxi driver knows the whole of London. And before he gets his cabbie's license he must just tour the city street by street, for months, then take a comprehensive exam.

So it is with many big cities, some much younger than London. They just spread out, pushed by the demands for residential, business, or industrial space. Like spilled water, they expanded in all directions. Today in New York, even a native-born Manhattanite despairs of finding his way around Brooklyn. In Chicago, a North Sider rarely ventures into the South Side without a street-guide in his pocket.

Planned Cities

There are a few cities, however, that were created whole out of nothing in modern times. And they were built strictly by the book according to detailed plans that will also control future growth. Two such American cities are **100** Columbia, Maryland, and Reston, Virginia.

The prime example of a city planned and built from scratch in the twentieth century is Brasília, the new capital of Brazil. Brasília was the brain child of Brazil's President Juscelino Kubitschek, in office from 1955 to 1960. Kubitschek, like other Brazilian leaders, was concerned that most of Brazil's people were crammed into its seacoast cities. Rio de Janeiro, then the nation's capital and its second-largest city, occupies a breathtaking site on the Atlantic coast. Sao Paulo, second largest city in the twin American continents, is very near the coast.

This meant that the vast stretches of Brazil's interior remained unpopulated and undeveloped. The nation's riches in timber, minerals, and hydroelectric power sources were untapped. So Kubitschek took the Brazilian bull by the horns. He decided to build a brand-new city in the Brazilian Highlands, 600 miles northwest of Rio de Janeiro. The site was plumb in the middle of the wilderness, on land that had not even been plowed.

Opened for business in 1960, Brasília was an architect's delight and a planner's dream. Its public buildings, monuments, and high-rise apartment complexes were magnificently modern. Access roads fed into its streets with no traffic lights. Every feature seemed logical, reasonable, and right.

Silent Streets

But for its first decade and longer, Brasília seemed all wrong to the people brought there to live and to work in government offices. It was a city, all right, but it wasn't a community. Brasília was brassy and beautiful, but it had about as much "soul" as a motel room.

For it is people and their history of habitation that turn a city from a collection of streets and buildings into a community. It is people who give a city life and character and personality. And brand-new tailor-made Brasília didn't have those qualities for a long time. Now, happily, Brasília is beginning to feel like home to its residents. They don't rush back to Rio or Sao Paulo at every opportunity. Instead, they visit, picnic, and enjoy one another's company.

In the U.S. and around the world today, the bigger the city, the bigger the lure. For decades now, the cities have drained the rural areas of their young and younger persons. At least seven out of 10 Americans now live in cities and towns.

"The farm (or small town) is a great place to be from," ex-ruralites say, "but city life is the life for me." Once they've settled in the city, few ever return to the country to live. They may retreat as far as the suburbs. But they first make sure that good roads and fast commuter trains provide quick trips to jobs, shopping, and entertainment in the city.

A big city offers its riches with lavish generosity. Its shops and stores are stuffed with a magnificent variety of wares. Its galleries and libraries are crammed full of great art and fascinating books. Its tall office buildings house every kind of business and professional service. Its theatres and concert halls present noted performers.

Neighborhoods

But a big city is also a place where people live and die, where their biographies are written on the walls of their houses and apartments, and on the streets they cross, on the buses they ride. And no matter how big the city, it is also a community—or rather a series of communities called neighborhoods.

A neighborhood is fairly self-sufficient, fairly self-contained. It has houses, apartments, shops, supermarkets, schools, churches, perhaps a hospital and a branch of the public library. It may very likely have a neighborhood association with some political clout.

Above all, a neighborhood is a familiar place to its inhabitants, an extension of the home itself. It is the city made small, the city reduced to community, a part of the city that a resident can become part of.

True, a neighborhood may become a segregated island within the city. A neighborhood may become segregated by choice, a place where an ethnic/religious group congregates to share and support their common interests. Or the segregation may be forced, as in a neighborhood where blacks or Puerto Ricans or white Appalachians live because they are not welcome elsewhere.

In some inner-city neighborhoods, the poor of all colors and races are segregated. This presents special problems, because many of the new manufacturing jobs are being offered by plants which have moved to the outskirts of suburbs. The poor have no cars, bus service from city to suburb is inadequate, and housing in the suburb is too costly for the inner-city poor. They can't find work in the city, and the suburb job is out of reach.

Thus the city presents two sides. One is rich, rewarding, magnificent. The other is bleak. Which one do you want? Which one do you deserve? Which one will you get?

What Do You Think? _____

1. What advantages might there be to new planned cities? What disadvantages?
2. What lessons can Brasília provide for planners?
3. What are the neighborhoods in your city? What do they add to city life?

---

3. The Case for Planning*

Hubert Humphrey, former Vice President of the United States and currently a Senator from Minnesota, is a strong proponent of planning and has introduced legislation in the Senate designed to facilitate a national planning process.

*Hubert H. Humphrey, *The Futurist,* December 1972.

Shall we "design" or "resign" ourselves to our nation's future?

That is the basic question underlying decisions we make today in determining what kind of nation we want to create or leave for future generations.

For what we do—or fail to do—today clearly commits and fixes future patterns of life in this nation as well as on this planet earth.

We can no longer afford the luxury of approaching the future of our nation—and its relationship to the rest of the world—haphazardly.

A few years back, we learned almost overnight that the world we live in had shrunk to such a size that men on one side of the earth could completely destroy men on the opposite side within 30 minutes through new and devastating means of modern warfare.

More recently we have come to realize that even the natural resources of this earth and of our nation are indeed finite, and in many cases threatened with total depletion.

And today we are approaching a new realization, one which was stated so eloquently by Barbara Ward and Rene Dubos in their recently published book: *Only One Earth.*

The establishment of a desirable human environment implies more than the maintenance of ecological equilibrium, the economical management of natural resources, and the control of the forces that threaten biological and mental health. Ideally, it requires also that social groups and individuals be provided with the opportunity to develop ways of life and surroundings of their own choice. Man not only survives and functions in his environment, he shapes it and he is shaped by it.

* * * * *

As of today, our nation still lacks those processes and mechanisms needed by government at all levels, and by individual citizens to develop and choose alternative futures.

As we approach our nation's bicentennial, it is not only appropriate, but essential that we look anew at the question of what kind of future we are now creating for ourselves and future generations by our decisions—or lack of decisions—as opposed to what we should be doing to move more toward a goal of human relationships based upon the Greek idea of "balance," of moderation, of "nothing too much."

Growth is seen by many as the opposite of stability, yet both are desired. Novelty is prized, but man is overwhelmed by too much change. Technology is both feared and indispensable.

Liberty versus tranquility, defense versus welfare, present versus future, are dichotomous[1] terms that have expressed American goals since the beginning of our Republic.

Our challenge then is to reach out for the "balance" in human relationships that many of us believe to be attainable between conflict and cooperation,

[1]Opposing.

between growth and stability, between individual free choice and common good, between technology and social responsibility, between economic needs and environmental protection, between urban and rural, between the old and new, and between national policy and state and local policy planning and development.

But how and through what means can we reach out for that balance?

What mechanisms and processes do we now have that will permit and encourage us to develop the policies and plans that will be needed if we are to create, to design and to shape our nation's future human environment?

I suggest to you that there are none, at least not any explicitly designed to deal with our nation's long range future.

We have no institution, process or mechanism today that is dedicated to or concerned with the consequences of the rapid and potent changes in opportunities resulting from the onrush of science and technology.

We have no national effort today concerned with the need for better techniques or measurement to help our society answer for itself the classic questions posed by Abraham Lincoln in his House Divided speech, which I wish to quote:

"If we could first know where we are, and whither we are tending, we could then better judge what to do and how to do it."

What Do You Think? _____

Mr. Humphrey argues strongly for better planning. Which of his arguments are most persuasive?

---

4. When Planning Doesn't Work

Sometimes plans go wrong; projects are completed and people, rather than rejoicing, begin to voice discontent at what has happened. Something went wrong, something didn't get considered, and perhaps the project has to be destroyed or substantially modified—at considerable expense to the taxpayers.

An Unwanted Expressway*

Build an expressway? It happens all the time. But tear one down?

In the 1950's irate San Franciscans stopped the elevated, waterfront section of the Embarcadero Freeway while under construction. Since then the

*David Holmstrom, "A City Tries to Lose a Freeway," *Christian Science Monitor.* Reprinted by permission from *The Christian Science Monitor.* Copyright © 1974 by The Christian Science Publishing Society. All rights reserved.

hulking band of concrete has ended abruptly in the air, hung over the waterfront.

Now, official sentiment is gathering momentum here to have the multimillion dollar structure demolished. If the structure does go down—approximately a mile long strip—it would mark the first time a freeway was destroyed in a state where freeways have been as dominant as gas stations.

But it would not signal the beginning of a trend.

The catch is that while the state has said it has no objections to razing the structure, it has another section planned in the same general area to link up with the Oakland Bay Bridge.

As it stands today the Embarcadero does come to an abrupt end, but two lanes lead off the freeway into downtown San Francisco.

In 1970 the State Division of Highways said it would cost more than $300 million to demolish an indefinite length of the freeway above and beyond the waterfront strip. By comparison, the Golden Gate Bridge cost $38 million to build in the 1930's.

Thomas Lammers, the district transportation director, said that the freeway produces "100,000 person trips a day" into the financial district of San Francisco.

"Whatever change is made will have to take into account the desire of 100,000 people to reach work," he said. He estimated that it would take "four to five years" to tear down the section and at the same time provide alternative traffic means.

County Supervisor Diane Feinstein wants the Embarcadero brought down because its absence would "provide additional open space to developers" in relation to construction already planned for the waterfront area.

She wants the state to provide an analysis of the demolition costs including a replacement underground traffic way with separate transit only lanes.

Mrs. Feinstein is a member of the Bay Conservation and Development Commission which recently set up a special waterfront advisory committee to tackle the delicate issue of development along the city's waterfront.

All 15 members of the commission said they want the freeway demolished not only for aesthetic reasons but also to release property currently shadowed underneath it.

What the state is proposing to do—with or without the Embarcadero—is create a 1.2-mile loop of freeway a little farther south of where the Embarcadero ends. The loop-94 feet wider than the Embarcadero—would connect Interstate 280 to the Oakland Bay Bridge. This section of freeway would be half as high as the Embarcadero.

Construction is scheduled to begin in 1975 with the opening date set at 1978. But the adamant initial rejection of the loop by the committee indicates that any proposal has a rough road ahead of it. An environmental impact statement is being drafted.

"It's a monster," said Dwight Steele, a Sierra Club member on the commission, referring to the State's new plan.

"It could become another Embarcadero," said another commission member remembering the legions of San Franciscans who turned out to stop the Embarcadero in the 1950's. Then the protest focused on the aesthetic ruination accompanying the freeway.

The commission did vote to consider three general planning concepts to guide them, two of which surprisingly included a still standing Embarcadero Freeway. "I'm glad we are proceeding cautiously," said commission chairman William Evers. I don't want to be accused of firing from the hip."

The irony is that few people agree on just where the "Embarcadero Freeway" begins. Everyone knows where it ends—like a cliff hanging over the end of Broadway. The term "Embarcadero" refers often to the waterfront area, and to the street of the same name that runs beneath the freeway.

To demolish the "Embarcadero Freeway" would take a preliminary agreement by officials as to what and where the freeway begins as Highway 101 swings into San Francisco from its coastal route and blends into the city skyline.

An End to a Housing Project

Still another instance of poor planning occurred in St. Louis. As a result, the Pruitt-Igoe housing development was built in the mid-1950's. Because it was a failure, part of the project was destroyed in 1973 and much of the rest of it will be renovated.

A hush settles over Building C-15 at the sprawling Pruitt-Igoe housing complex in the bowels of St. Louis worst slums. Some 152 bundles of dynamite are planted in the basement and first floors of the 11-story building. A bullhorn intones: Four, Three, Two, One. Then a chain of muffled explosions timed in two-second intervals generates a vacuum-like effect, sucking the reinforced steel and concrete walls neatly toward the center and reducing to rubble what was once home for 200 families.

Ironically, Building C-15 has been part of a housing project only 18 years old, a project that fell into disrepair soon after it won a 1958 architectural design award; plagued today by crime, poor maintenance and city-federal buck-passing. Pruitt-Igoe is "the Monster," the housing of last resort for the poorest of poor blacks. About 50 percent (1918) of its 2367 units are vacant. By blowing up several of its 33 buildings (at a demolition cost of about $67,000 each) and by slicing others from 11 to 4 stories, St. Louis housing authorities plan to decrease Pruitt-Igoe's housing density from an unwieldy 48 units per acre to 20. These and other ingenious innovations, they hope, will attract store tenants.

But to other St. Louisians, Pruitt-Igoe is a sin of the fathers that cannot be expiated through clever experiments of the sort. These observers believe the entire complex should be totally destroyed to end an environmental mistake by presumably well intentioned, but ill-informed urban planners. And so the project's future teeters in the balance. So likewise teeters the future of St. Louis

low-income blacks, waiting in vain for some 50,000 units of modern new housing. Since February, only one federally subsidized project of 76 units has been approved for St. Louis by the U.S. Department of Housing and Urban Development (HUD) under the newest policies addressed to the housing crisis. During that same period, however, HUD has approved housing developments in the all-white and three predominantly-white towns outside of St. Louis.

Although the housing crisis symbolized by Pruitt-Igoe was solely St. Louis centered, it could be of local concern too. But there is the 1,206 unit Stella Wright project in Newark, N.J., Cabrini Green (3,600 units) in Chicago and Hunters Point (1,346 units) in San Francisco. All of these projects are high-rise silos stacking human beings like so many ears of corn. All have little if any play areas, poor maintenance and even worse security. All are plagued with vandalism and crime. All are infested with rats, dope addicts, drunks and derelicts.

The monotony of these grim facts repeats itself in city after city across the nation. All are critically short of livable, low-income housing. And therein lies the detonator for potentially explosive confrontations between poor blacks concentrated in central cities where 40 percent of the housing is dilapidated and rings of affluent whites in the suburbs where 80 percent of all new housing is being built and where 80 percent of all new industrial jobs created in the 1960's are located. The countdown in the cities has been trickling off for more than 20 years during which all sorts of federal laws have prohibited, at least on paper, discrimination in Federally assisted housing programs. Unfortunately, lack of vigorous enforcement has drastically reduced the effectiveness of these laws.

What Do You Think? _____

1. Many citizens of San Francisco still want the Embarcadero Freeway torn down. What might be arguments for and against tearing it down?
2. What can be done to ensure that future Pruitt-Igoe's do not occur and that housing for the poor is adequate and humane?

_____

5. Technology and City Life*

One of the newest methods of transportation may result in individual rapid transit. The following story shows how this development may effect our future.

Personal Rapid Transit—A Definition

Personal Rapid Transit is the class of fixed-guideway systems in which automated vehicles no larger than small automobiles carry people and/or goods non-stop between any pairs of stations in a network of slim guideways which may serve major activity centers, airports, etc., or may span an entire urban area. PRT vehicles are occupied by a single individual or by people traveling together and may be captive to the guideway or have the capability of operating on both the guideway and street systems.

The problem of urban transportation can only worsen in future years if we continue to rely on the automobile. New systems capable of attracting at least half the trips made into a city must be developed by 1990, and conventional transit technology falls far short of this goal.

In the United States, Western Europe and Japan such systems are being developed. In the United States, where serious planning in many cities is well under way, the system has become known as Personal Rapid Transit—PRT. As this technology advances, all of its implications for society must be carefully assessed.

To attract automobile drivers to public transit without coercion, the transit trip must be faster than the auto trip for a significant number of trips typically made by urban residents. Transit vehicles will have to travel on an exclusive guideway above or below the street level. Accessibility and convenience will require an areawide network of interconnected guideways. An areawide network must not, however, be constructed all at once. It must be built gradually and with careful planning so that the social, economic and environmental impacts can be understood and accepted by the community.

The major innovation leading to PRT can be seen in the history of highway development. Decades ago, state highways were built around cities to speed up interstate travel. This led to the urban freeway, which attracted drivers in great numbers. Under unsaturated conditions the trip on a freeway is nonstop and a driver starts and stops only for reasons connected with his own trip. The trip is accomplished in minimum time with minimum frustration and maximum comfort.

In order to have a rapid transit system with the nonstop character of the urban freeway, planners have developed the concept of a system of fixed guideways in which the stations are on by-pass tracks off the main line. The off-line station permits vehicles to wait for people—not people for vehicles. Maximum capacity is obtained if all acceleration and deceleration maneuvers associated with leaving and entering the stations are accomplished on the by-pass tracks.

Small vehicles have two primary advantages:

1. The guideways can be light, low cost, and relatively inconspicuous. It appears now that the guideway so dominates the overall capital cost that the minimum-size vehicle leads also to the minimum overall system cost even though more vehicles are necessary.

2. The option of truly personal service is available. This means that each cab is occupied only by persons traveling together, and that it is unnecessary to travel with strangers. Many conversations with citizens about PRT have led us to believe that such privacy is a very important feature. In the personal cabs, each passenger would have a seat. This would not only increase comfort, and

hence, patronage, but would also permit the acceleration and deceleration to be approximately double that tolerable if passengers were allowed to stand. As a result, ramp lengths would be cut approximately in half.

To increase system flexibility the vehicles can be pallets, that is, moving platforms on which pods for carrying people or goods or even dual mode— a combination of automobile and PRT—and permits door-to-door transportation.

Safe and reliable control of a large number of small vehicles switching in and out of stations and from line to line requires use of advanced techniques of automatic control and reliability engineering developed during the past two decades. When compared with manual control, automatic control has the advantage that the labor costs of transit are considerably reduced. Service can continue 24 hours a day. By using an interconnected system of one-way lines, a city can nearly double the percentage of urban land area within walking distance of stations for a given investment. Use of one-way lines also means that the visual impact of the system on a given street is reduced.

Conventional transit makes people wait for vehicles. With PRT, the vehicles wait at off-line stations for people. Computer studies have shown that at rush periods, PRT systems can be designed so that the wait period is no more than 30 seconds to one minute. Conventional transit requires people to stop and start many times between the origin and destination for reasons unrelated to the purpose of the individual trip. PRT provides nonstop trips to all riders, whereas conventional transit requires them to transfer from line to line. With PRT, a computer automatically transfers a vehicle from one line to another according to the rider's destination. Conventional transit requires the user to master complex and frequently changing routes and schedules. With PRT every station is connected with every other station by a nonstop trip. The traveller goes to the nearest station, where he is assured of immediate nonstop service to any destination in the network. Conventional transit is crowded and impersonal. With PRT, the trip is taken in privacy with one's own traveling companions. Personal security is thereby substantially increased.

With conventional transit, it is expensive to provide frequent service during off-peak hours, hence there is no service at all between midnight and 6 A.M. With PRT, it costs nothing to store vehicles in stations, waiting for people 24 hours a day. Conventional transit offers too little to attract people from autos, but PRT provides a level of service considerably superior to the automobile for many types of trips.

Before we begin to think seriously about the implications of a technology, we must believe the ideas behind the hardware are sound. PRT is at a point where a straight-forward period of engineering development can bring it to maturity. What PRT needs is exposure to public opinion.

PRT Around the World

The Department of Transportation last October announced that $11 million in Federal funds will be invested in a demonstration project with five people mover vehicles running on a one-mile guideway in Denver, Colorado.

Eventually, Denver's Regional Transportation District is expected to develop a full scale system with 500 vehicles and five miles of guideway between Mile High Stadium and downtown Denver. The initial tests on the one-mile stretch are expected to take place in 1975.

* * * * *

Architects making the first comprehensive impact study of PRT in an old established city used the West End of London as a guinea pig and came up with the conclusion that many London streets would actually look better with the addition of a PRT guideway.

Under consideration was Cabtrack, a system using driverless, electrically powered four-seater vehicles. The architects used a method of photo-montage to obtain vivid visual impressions of what Cabtrack would do to London. Their report stated that Cabtrack would be "a public transport system of reliability, convenience and comfort and a powerful tool for conversation, restoring to us those parts of our cities in which we most wish to linger and look.

* * * * *

A two-mile loop system of PRT will be built in Toronto in time for the Canadian National Exposition of May 1975. Construction will begin next summer.

Semi-finalists in an international competition for construction of the project are the Ford Motor Company of the United States, Hawker-Siddeley of Canada and Krauss-Maffei of West Germany.

* * * * *

A Personal Rapid Transit system using the principles of electomagnetism for levitation, guidance and propulsion will be tested in Munich in 1973 by a West German Company, Krauss-Maffei.

The 12-passenger vehicle will be suspended, guided, propelled and switched by electromagnetic forces. Neither the vehicle or the track will have any moving parts; the switches will be solid state devices.

* * * * *

A PRT system called Spartaxi is being planned for Gothenburg, Sweden, where the first test track will open in 1974.

The system will use small four to six passenger vehicles traveling on a main guideway at high speed separate sidetrack stations where passengers will alight and entrain. The system will be controlled by computers.

* * * * *

Component testing for West Germany's Cabin Taxi System was scheduled to be completed in Munich in 1972 and a test track for prototypes will operate in 1973.

Vehicles for two adults and one child will travel on steel guideways. The two-guideways are superimposed so that vehicles traveling in one direction are suspended beneath the guideway and those traveling in the other direction are mounted on top.

A larger experimental network to study user acceptance is planned for 1974 and the first public network will go into operation in 1976. This system is sponsored by the West German Government and Messerschmitt and Demag.

Japan's new Computer Controlled Vehicle System, developed by the Ministry of Industrial Trade and Industry, will have its first trial run in 1973.

The system consists of small, electrically powered, automatically controlled vehicles operating on a dense network of guideways with off-line stations. The vehicles seat two adults with a supplemental rear seat for children or packages. Main passenger seats face the rear and air bags will be used for passenger protection in the event of a collision.

Operating speed on express links will be 60 kilometers per hour, on slow speed links, 40 kilometers per hour.

What Do You Think? _____

1. PRT has attracted worldwide attention. What are the principal merits of such a transportation system?
2. How well would a PRT system work in your community? How would you go about getting consideration of such a proposal?

6. Citizen Participation in Decision Making*

A critical problem for planners and elected officials is how they can involve citizens making important decisions. Fresno, California, has developed one method for generating citizen participation.

Like so many "other sides of the tracks," West Fresno was left behind as neighboring communities developed. Always an area inhabited by immigrants and ethnic minorities, it deteriorated sharply after World War II and nearly became a black ghetto in the 1960s.

Although fortunate in being physically unified—quite literally, it is on the other side of the tracks and freeway from Fresno—West Fresno is seriously divided by municipal, school and special-district boundaries.

Since 1968, large redevelopment and model-cities projects have materially improved living conditions, but the prospect of advancing them to a point at which West Fresno can stand alone is slim because of prospective reductions in federal grants. Indeed, can any community stand on its own, even with adequate funds, unless its people have sufficient unity and incentive to affect their own condition? Urban renewal will continue to fail in its larger purpose until the people themselves can carry a major part of the long-term responsibility. . . .

To give strength to self-renewal and clearer focus to the human dimension, "West Fresno: A Plan for Community Development" departs from previous efforts in a number of ways, especially in defining a precise role for "community development." Rather than relying entirely upon the segregated and socially irrelevant land-use categories—residential, industrial, commercial, transportation, public facilities and arbitrary densities—the plan emphasizes the community theme and relates urban functions to the only valid reason for the existence of cities: the individual. . . .

The concept of community reflects two historic developments whose burdens now weigh heavily on cities. First, although I do not imply that urban plans are consciously less than humane, it is important to recognize that for nearly two centuries the processes of modernization have shifted the focus from viable small communities to huge, depersonalized metropolitan areas. The vital core of the former was social; the basis of the latter is economic. Today's slums are partly the result of that fact. The premise of the current view of community development is that we can be as decisive and organized in social development as we have in economic development.

Second, our federal system in the beginning concentrated on national and state governments, since grass-roots democracy was then functioning well

*Reprinted with permission from "The Community's Role in Urban Planning," by Kenneth R. Schneider, in the Fall 1973 issue of *Cry California,* published by California Tomorrow, San Francisco.

locally. After nearly 200 years of this emphasis, however, urban, industrial and bureaucratic growth have all but erased direct personal involvement in local government. City Hall is distant. The citizen has no ready means of organizing with his neighbors. Both the problems and the organizations for their solution are beyond human scale and out of his reach. As a consequence, there is little local identity, meager cooperation, and a pervading sense of helplessness.

Against this background, the community envisioned by the West Fresno plan may be examined.

"The heart of this plan," the report states, "is the development of a strong, unified West Fresno Community made up of 11 vigorous neighborhoods." The community's population could increase from 22,000 to about 55,000, while the neighborhoods could vary from 3,500 to 6,000 each. Organized around the service area of the elementary school, in the classic formula first proposed in 1929 by the late author, educator and social planner, Clarence Perry, the neighborhood would be large enough to support a good range of services and activities, but small enough for individual citizens to take a decisive part in its affairs.

The community as a whole would have its own wider range of services and activities in a multi-functional complex within the most central neighborhood. The loss in personal association at a population scale of 50,000 is offset by a greater breadth of civic potential: a high school, a health center, more specialized shopping, broader community facilities, and housing of a more cosmopolitan character. To the extent these can function as a unified whole through multiple-use facilities, the community center will perform its most basic role: to promote more effective public dialogue, generate consensus, and build the leadership necessary to develop a true community of interest. . . .

It is becoming recognized as inadequate to speak of developing public services for people. We need instead to provide a framework within which people can organize to pursue their own aspirations, be they athletics, art, archeology, soaring, philosophy, winemaking or needle work.

What prospers in a society is what is nurtured. We have encouraged consumption and this has pushed us headlong into energy and pollution crises. What should now be fostered is the boundless potential of people through their experience and interaction in local areas. . . .

The idea of community, as evolved in West Fresno, supposes that each neighborhood will serve as a separate—though not unrelated—base from which to evolve its own traditions of solid distinctiveness. Preserving ethnic identity also appears to be a legitimate and highly valid goal, although civil rights and the access of minorities to the broadest advantages of society currently overshadow consideration of such diversity. In any case, local traditions —those which lie at the base of diverse and distinctive behavior—must evolve in their own terms. The planner's responsibility is to build the broadest framework within which this can occur.

For the individual, there is another kind of diversity. Traditionally, there have been two major focal points for human behavior: the family, which is intimate and communal; and the community, which is familiar and interper-   **113** sonal. It is the genius of modern man to have created a third, the cosmopolitan world of universities, corporations, bureaucracy and specialized professionalism, which is basically anonymous. But in so doing, the modern urban world left the community fragmented and virtually nonexistent. Yet all three—the family, the community and the metropolis—form a foundation that can optimize personal, social and economic opportunities.

The reestablished role for community, therefore, is to fill the middle void we have created, to act as a base for participation in the cosmopolitan world, and to provide a framework for strengthening the family.

Community is valid on practical as well as social grounds. As community development in other countries has demonstrated, it reaches people in the setting of their lives where both the problems and their solutions rest. As people develop faith and confidence in their own ability to develop their neighborhoods, they move closer to their highest potential.

What Do You Think? _____

1. Why is it important to involve people in community decision making?
2. What are the vehicles for such involvement in your community?
3. What is your response to the Fresno plan? What do you see as its strengths and weaknesses?

ACTIVITIES FOR INVOLVEMENT

1. Choose a chairman and a committee to unify the various reports the class or committees have made as previous activities. Write a summary statement identifying what the class believes to be of highest priority in your city, or the city nearest you. The final plan should be submitted to the entire class for ratification and amendment. Once the entire process is completed, copies should be given to the local planning commission, at a meeting of that commission.

2. After the final report is adopted prepare a debate on the following question: "Resolved: That city planning commissions be given the power to put their plans into effect without approval by the local law-making body."

3. Now that most of the work on this unit has been completed, begin a campaign to get students included as advisory members to local commissions and boards. See the mayor and other officials and get ther endorsement. Make a list of all those whom you must contact and who can exert influence for what you want.

4. In small groups discuss the future of your city and other cities in the United States. Keep no notes and make the atmosphere informal. Which of your city's problems concern you? What can you, as an individual, do about these problems? What are you going to do?

5. Contact the department of urban studies at your local college or university. Ask one of the professors to review your work and visit your classroom.

6. As a final project, form a committee to look into the question of jobs in the field of urban planning and social services. This should become a part of your final report.

BIBLIOGRAPHY
For Further Study

BOOKS

ABRAMS, CHARLES • *The City Is The Frontier* • New York: Harper Colophon Books, 1965.

ARANGO, JORGE • *The Urbanization of the Earth* • Boston: Beacon Press, 1970.

BLUMENFELD, HANS • *The Modern Metropolis* • Cambridge, Mass.: MIT Press, 1967.

BROWN, CLAUDE • *Manchild in the Promised Land* • New York: Signet Books, 1966. (paperback)

CARSON, RACHEL • *Silent Spring* • Boston: Houghton Mifflin, 1962.

CLARK, KENNETH • *Dark Ghetto* • New York: Harper & Row, 1965.

CLAY, GRADY • *Close-Up: How to Read the American City* • New York: Praeger, 1974.

CONOT, ROBERT • *Rivers of Blood, Years of Darkness* • New York: Bantam Books, 1967. (paperback)

CUNNINGHAM, JAMES • *The Resurgent Neighborhood* • Notre Dame, Ind.: Fides Publishers, 1965.

DAHINDEN, JUSTUS • *Urban Structures for the Future,* • New York: Praeger, 19xx. 1972.

DAVIS, KINGLSEY (compiler) • *Cities: Their Origin, Growth & Human Impact* • San Francisco: W. H. Freeman, 1973.

DOXIADES, KONSTANTINOS • *Ecumenopolis: The Settlement of the Future* • Athens Technical Organization, Athens Center of Ekistics, 1967.

DRAKE, ST. CLAIR, and HORACE R. GAYTON • *Black Metropolis* (Vols I & II) • New York: Harper Torchbooks, 1945. (paperback)

Editors of Scientific American • *Cities* • New York: Alfred A. Knopf, 1965.

GOODMAN, ROBERT • *After the Planners* • New York: Simon & Schuster,19xx.1971.

GORDON, MITCHELL • *Sick Cities* • Baltimore, Md.: Penguin Books, 1945. (paperback)

GORDON, RICHARD E., KATHERINE GORDON, and MAX GUNTHER • *The Split Level Trap* • New York: Dell Publishing Co., 1967. (paperback)

GUTMAN, ROBERT (compiler) • *Neighborhood, City and Metropolis: An Integrated Reader in Urban Sociology* • New York: Random House. 1970.

HANDLIN, OSCAR • *The Uprooted* • New York: Grosset and Dunlap, 1951.

HARRINGTON, MICHAEL • *The Other America: Poverty in the United States* • Baltimore, Md.: Penguin Books, 1963. (paperback)

HOOVER, EDGAR A., and RAYMOND VERNON • *Anatomy of a Metropolis* • Garden City, N. Y.: Doubleday Anchor, 1962. (paperback)

JACOBS, JANE • *The Death and Life of Great American Cities* • New York: Vintage, 1961. (paperback)

KEATS, JOHN • *The Insolent Chariots* • Philadelphia: J. G. Lippincott, 1958.

LAURENTS, ARTHUR • *West Side Story* • New York: Random House, 1957.
Le CORBUSIER • *The City of Tomorrow* • Cambridge, Mass.: The MIT Press, 1971.
Le CORBUSIER • *Looking at City Planning* • New York: Grossman, 1971.
LINDSAY, JOHN • *The City* • New York: W. W. Norton & Co., 1970.
LOWE, JEANNE • *Cities in a Race with Time: Progress and Poverty in America's Renewing Cities* • New York: Vintage, 1968. (paperback)
McGEE, T. G. • *The Urbanization Process in the Third World* • London: G. Bell & Sons, 1971.
McQUADE • *Cities Fit to Live in, and How We Can Make Them Happen* • New York: Macmillan, 1971.
MILLER, WARREN • *The Cool World* • Greenwich, Conn.: Fawcett World Library, 1964.
MOYNIHAN, DANIEL PATRICK, and NATHAN GLAZER • *Beyond the Melting Pot* • Cambridge, Mass.: MIT Press, 1963.
MUMFORD, LEWIS • *The City in History* • New York: Harcourt, Brace & World, 1961.
MUMFORD, LEWIS • *The Highway and the City* • New York: New American Library, 1962.
MUMFORD, LEWIS • *The Urban Prospect* • New York: Harcourt, Brace & World, 1968.
OWEN, WILFRED • *The Accessible City* • Washington, D.C.: The Brookings Institution, 1972.
ROBSON, WILLIAM (ed.) • *Great Cities of the World: Their Government, Politics and Planning* • Beverly Hills, Calif: Sage Publications, 1972.
SILBERMAN, CHARLES E. • *Crisis in Black and White* • New York: Random House, 1964.
SPECTORSKY, A. C. • *The Exurbanites* • Philadelphia: J. B. Lippincott, 1955.
STEFFENS, LINCOLN • *The Shame of the Cities* • New York: Hill and Wang, 1957.
THOMAS, PIRI • *Down These Mean Streets* • New York: Alfred A. Knopf, 1967.
VERNON, RAYMOND • *Metropolis 1985* • New York: Doubleday Anchor, 1965. (paperback)
WEAVER, ROBERT C. • *The Urban Complex* • New York: Doubleday Anchor, 1966.
WRIGHT, FRANK LLOYD • *The Industrial Revolution Runs Away* • New York: Horizon Press, 1964.
WRIGHT, NATHAN JR. • *Black Power and Urban Unrest* • New York: Hawthorn Books, 1967.

SPECIAL REPORTS

The Exploding Metropolis • The Editors of Fortune, Doubleday Anchor, 1958.
Report of the National Advisory Commission on Civil Disorders • (The Kerner Report), 1968.
A Time to Listen . . . A Time to Act • Report of the U.S. Commission on Civil Rights, 1967.

ARTICLES

"Big City Woes as the Mayors See Them" • *U.S. News & World Report,* July 3, 1972.
"Black Takeover of the U.S. Cities" • A. Poinsett, *Ebony,* November 1970.

"Cities Are Finished" • S. Alsop, *Newsweek,* April 5, 1971.
"Cities in the Seventies" • *Senior Scholastic,* December 4, 1972.
"Cities on the Sea" • John Lear, *Saturday Review,* December 4, 1971.
"The City" • *Psychology Today,* August 1968.
"City: Symposium" • *Horizon,* Autumn 1972.
"The Conscience of the City" • *Daedalus,* Fall 1968.
"The Future Metropolis" • *Daedalus,* Winter 1961.
"Getting Bigger All the Time: U.S. Super-Cities" • *U.S. News & World Report,* July 11, 1973.
"The Negro and the Cities" • *Life,* March 8, 1968.
"No for No Growth: Petaluma California Case" • *Time,* February 18, 1974.
"Our Sick Cities" • *Look,* September 21, 1965.
"Squeezing Spread City: The Gasoline Shortage" • A. Downs, *The New York Times Magazine,* March 17, 1974.
"Three Mayors Speak of Their Cities" • *Ebony,* February 1974.
"Toward the Year 2000: Work in Progress" • *Daedalus,* Summer 1967.
"Urban Environment: Cities Made for People" • *Senior Scholastic,* February 8, 1971.
"The U.S. City" • *Life,* December 24, 1965.
"Where's the Best Place to Live?" • *Changing Times,* October 1972.

FILMS

The Battle of Newburgh (16 mm; B/W; 54 min; prod. NBC News) • NBC News white paper on the drastic methods suggested by Newburgh, New York, officials in an attempt to reduce payments to welfare recipients. The film explores the fallacies involved in the projected cuts.

Calcutta (16 mm; 115 min; color; 1968; prod. Pyramid Films) • A prize-winning documentary of the Indian city of Calcutta directed by Louis Halle. The population crisis of the city and its accompanying ecological disasters are portrayed.

The Changing City (12 min; color; prod. Churchill Films) • Deals with the effects on people of metropolitan living. The use of land and the renewal of old cities are discussed with special reference to the historical pattern of city growth.

Chicago—Midland Metropolis (22 min; color; 1963; prod. Encyclopaedia Britannica Films) • Why Chicago grew and became one of the great cities of the world. Discusses geography, immigration, and industrialization. Notes the changing demands of urban life.

Cities of the Future (25 min; color; CBS News for the "21st Century" Series; dist. McGraw-Hill Films) • Focuses on the creative planning now in progress to surmount current problems. Covers 12 cities around the globe.

The City (11 min; color; 1958; prod. Encyclopaedia Britannica Films) • Scenes of a complex city, including many types of buildings, neighborhoods, transportation facilities, suburban areas, and city government.

The City and Its Region (28 min; B/W; 1963; prod. Natl. Film Board of Canada; dist. Sterling Educational Films) • Examines how balance and harmony between city and countryside can be maintained or restored in today's metropolitan regions.

The City and the Future (28 min; B/W; 1963; prod. Natl. Film Board of Canada; dist. Sterling Educational Films) • Explains that cities must choose between low-grade urban sprawl or a new kind of regional city.

The City as Man's Home (28 min; B/W; 1963; prod. Natl. Film Board of Canada; dist.

Sterling Educational Films) • Examines how slums, public housing, suburbs, luxury apts. developed. Suggests ways to improve the quality of city life.

The City—Cars or People (28 min; B/W; 1963; prod. Natl. Film Board of Canada; dist. Sterling Educational Films) • Studies the problem of how to make the city accessible without allowing transportation to make it congested and uninhabitable. Shows problems and solutions of several cities.

The City—Heaven and Hell (28 min; B/W; 1963; prod. Natl. Film Board of Canada; dist. Sterling Educational Films) • Outlines the creative and destructive natures of the city in history. Covers elements that caused the creation of the first cities and forces that now threaten the city.

City Series (Stirling Films) • Six films with Lewis Mumford illustrating and discussing the problems of cities, including transportation, downtown, regional planning, and the future.

I Wonder Why (6 min; B/W; 1966; dist. McGraw-Hill Films) • A photographic essay depicting the thoughts of a young black girl.

Panoramic Impressions of Old New York (11 min; B/W; 1903; prod. Black Hawk Studios) • New York City at the turn of the century. Its problems, its changing skyline, and its growth.

Photography and the City (12 min; color; 1972; prod. Charles Eames) • How to use photography to capture the city. Discusses many uses of photography.

The Problem with Water Is People (30 min; color and B/W; prod. NBC News; dist. McGraw-Hill Films) • Examines the potential crisis in the nation's most vital natural resource—water.

A Trip from Chicago (25 min; color; prod. CBS News for the "21st Century" Series; dist. McGraw-Hill Films) • Investigates the means by which people and goods will be transported in the near future. Covers air, land, and sea craft—some operative, some in the design stages.

The Uprooted Nation (22 min; color; 1965; prod. Churchill Films) • A close look at the long-term immigration patterns within the United States and their effect on individuals and communities. Utilizes the insights of city planners and demographers, among others.

Uptown: A Portrait of the South Bronx (27 min; B/W; 1965; dist. McGraw-Hill) • A picture of a disadvantaged community within New York City and the way of life of the people.